Dover and Folkestone
During the Great War

'WAITING FOR YOU IN 'BLIGHTY'!

Blighty! A Fred Spurgin illustration reminding the British soldier of home.

Dover and Folkestone During the Great War

Michael and Christine George

Pen & Sword
MILITARY

First published in Great Britain in 2008 by
Pen & Sword Military
an imprint of
Pen & Sword Books Ltd
47 Church Street
Barnsley
South Yorkshire
S70 2AS

ISBN 978 1 84415 842 3

A CIP catalogue record for this book is
available from the British Library.

Printed and bound in Great Britain
by CPI UK

Pen & Sword Books Ltd incorporates the imprints of
Pen & Sword Aviation, Pen & Sword Family History, Pen & Sword Maritime,
Pen & Sword Military, Wharncliffe Local History, Pen & Sword Select,
Pen & Sword Military Classics, Leo Cooper, Remember When,
Seaforth Publishing and Frontline Publishing.

For a complete list of Pen & Sword titles please contact
PEN & SWORD BOOKS LIMITED
47 Church Street, Barnsley, South Yorkshire, S70 2AS, England
E-mail: enquiries@pen-and-sword.co.uk
Website: www.pen-and-sword.co.uk

Cover illustrations.
Front: Target Dover! A German illustration from 1915 showing an air raid on the town.
Back: Arrivals and Departures. A 1917 painting by artist Louis Raemaekers showing
activity at the RNAS Air station, Capel le Ferne, midway between Dover and Folkestone.

Contents

This book is dedicated to the Merchant Marine sailors and the fishermen
who served in the Dover Patrol during the Great War.

The Raemaekers' painting of Capel RNAS Station painted in July 1917.

Foreword by Allan Willett CMG, Lord Lieutenant of Kent, The Queen's Representative in the County

From the arrival of Julius Caesar through to the Battle of Britain fought in our skies, Kent has always been in the vanguard of the Nation. Winston Churchill aptly called it 'this glorious foreland of England ... the bulwark of its defence', and none can dispute its claim to be the Frontline County.

People speak of the Garden of England, but well before that our proud County was the *Guardian* of England. Our geographical position, essentially a peninsula shaped like the British bulldog's chin jutting out proudly into the Channel as if to deter invaders, has bequeathed us a unique history. We have been at centre stage for 2,000 years, and over the centuries the crucial importance of our Channel ports of Dover and Folkestone – on the short sea-invasion route from Continental Europe – was unrivalled.

Their role has never been more vital than during the Great War of 1914–1918. Both towns were subjected to bombardment from the sea, and suffered some of the first major air raids, an evil foretaste of what was to come in the Second World War. But, ever defiant, they took a leading part in winning victory as strategically situated bases from which to protect our shipping and to pour ever more Allied troops over to the Western Front. The whole area became an armed camp and the White Cliffs were a potent, poignant last symbol of home for all the young men who left these shores to die at sea or in the trenches – and a wonderfully welcome sight for those who made it home, to Blighty.

Sadly, with the passing of the generations who lived through those times, the enormous contribution of these Kentish ports has largely been forgotten – until now. Thanks to Michael and Christine George, the dramatic story of those climactic times is here brought to life. Importantly, and unusually, this book records not only the triumphs and disasters of the military conflict, but reveals – for the first time in any detail – what daily life was really like on the Home Front. It is a long overdue and fitting tribute to the great service and sacrifice of the ordinary people of our Channel ports in extraordinary times.

Abbreviations

At the end of each quotation from a contemporary source there appears a name. These are abbreviations of the sources listed below, full details of which appear in the bibliography.

[Jerrold]: Walter Jerrold, *Highways & Byways in Kent*

[Mitton]: G E Mitton, *The South-Eastern & Chatham and London, Brighton & South Coast Railways*

[Ward Lock Guide]: *A Pictorial and Descriptive Guide to Hythe, Sandgate and Folkestone* (Ward, Lock and Co. Ltd, 1914)

[Carlile]: J C Carlile, *Folkestone during the War 1914–1919*

[Jones]: John Jones, *Folkestone and the War*

[Coxon]: Lieutenant Commander Stanley Coxon, *Dover During the Dark Days*

Acknowledgements

We would like to thank everyone who has helped to bring this book to fruition. In the same way that during the Great War, for every aircraft that took to the air, or every ship that left port, there was not only the pilot or the captain, but many men and women working behind the scenes, so it has been here. They have done their best to set us on the right course; any errors in navigation are entirely the responsibility of the authors.

Especial thanks must go to Dennis Booth for material about his father, Clarence; Judy Seely for the information about William Meehan; Penny Hiatt, who allowed us to use the picture of Florence Rumsey; Susan Evans-Shaw, whose father, Captain James Evans, is featured; and David McDine for sharing with us the story of his uncle, William Poile. We are grateful to the Folkestone Heritage Museum for permission to reproduce the images of Folkestone Harbour and HMTS *Victoria* in Chapter 3. All other illustrations are from our own collection or in the public domain.

Finally, thanks to our editor, Rupert Harding, who has encouraged and chivvied us throughout our journey.

Introduction

As we approach the ninetieth anniversary of the end of the First World War, there will be some, only a few, who remember those days. For most of us, it is impossible to conceive what life was like then. We cannot understand what sense of duty led hundreds of thousands of young men to volunteer for the horror of trench warfare, then 'going over the top' into the teeth of chattering machine guns. Perhaps it was, as Kipling suggested:

> When they ask why we died
> Tell them, because our fathers lied.

Bookshop shelves groan under the weight of volumes covering, it seems, every aspect of the war. Most concentrate on the scenes of the fighting, with perhaps the greatest number devoted to that most horrific theatre of the war, the Western Front. There are very few books devoted to the Home Front and still fewer have described events and conditions along the area of coastline which, for centuries, has been known as the 'Gateway to the Kingdom'. As we shall discover, this was a remarkable area; it was the interface between Blighty, represented for so many by the white cliffs of Dover, and the noise, mud and death of the war. For many, the towns of south Kent were the last they were to see of their homeland, before finding a resting place in one of the vast war cemeteries of Belgium or northern France.

While the threat of invasion subsided after the German invasion of France and Flanders was halted on the Western Front, the protection of the coast and the cross-channel shipping routes from marauding enemy ships and submarines was critical. With the advent of manned flight, attack from the skies by Zeppelins and aircraft was an ever-present threat.

The transition from peace to war was sudden and uncompromising. The wide tree-lined boulevards of Folkestone were soon turned into muddy and potholed routes for the men, horses and machinery of war. The elegant Victorian and Edwardian homes were abandoned or taken over as billets and hospital annexes. Dover became a Restricted Area, essentially governed by martial law, with only those holding an official pass being allowed entry.

Our purpose in writing this book has been twofold. First, to tell the story of Britain's front line, where the sounds of gunfire from the front could often be heard, and where it was said a soldier could eat his breakfast in Folkestone and by lunchtime could be in the trenches. Secondly, we have tried to record as many experiences as possible of the men and women who lived through those years. Some of those people wrote books, often in words which we might today regard as quaint, perhaps even naive. It is said that a picture is worth a thousand words. One feature of Great War photography was the severe control by the British government. In comparison the Germans had few restrictions, and this means that many images from that war are of German origin. The British press often had to buy German photographs or improvise, using artists' impressions. On both sides of the conflict, the postcard was both an important means of communication between individuals, but also a powerful propaganda tool and we include a number of these, both British and German.

A word of explanation about how this book has been written. It is chronological, with the first chapter giving a broad picture of life as it was at the end of Queen Victoria's reign through the Edwardian period to the days of King George V. These are the years of peace, but with the spectre, for those who could see ahead, of war clouds on the horizon. A detailed examination of the war years then follows, when we look at many of the events, great and small, which occurred along this stretch of English coast. Finally, there is the return to peace and we look at how this was marked, from a humble street party in Folkestone, to the pomp surrounding the arrival of the Unknown Warrior at Dover.

Chapter 1

The Last Days of Peace

The decade before the outbreak of war saw the transition from the somewhat sombre days at the end of Victoria's reign to the brighter prospects of the new Edwardian era. The class system was still entrenched and women were still without the vote, despite the suffragette movement. The British Empire remained the jewel in the crown and the source of much of the country's wealth. But things were changing. Both France and Germany were looking to expand their empires and were increasing the size of their armies and navies to support their expansionist policies. Britain was determined to keep her place as ruler of the world's oceans, and ever larger warships were sliding down the slipways at the country's dockyards. For centuries the enemy had been France, but, with the signing of the Entente Cordiale in 1904, that had changed. The threat was seen to be from Germany, where Queen Victoria's grandson, Kaiser Wilhelm II, was at the helm.

Welcome to the Kaiser. In 1902 Queen Victoria's grandson visited Shorncliffe Camp. It rained all day.

For the man in the street, there was little evidence of the coming conflict. The Kaiser himself had been to England in 1902 and had reviewed the troops at Shorncliffe army camp at Folkestone. The very notion of a world war was impossible to imagine. The last one had ended in 1815, with the final defeat of Napoleon. There had been many conflicts since then: the Crimean War, the Indian Mutiny, the Zulu Wars and, most recently, the Boer Wars. They had all taken place far away and, although history tells us how badly managed they were, the population at home were told only of glorious victories.

Peace and prosperity seemed to be assured, especially with exciting new technology: the motor car was gradually becoming more fashionable and some blacksmiths were making the transition to motor mechanics. Most exciting of all was the development of flight. Louis Blériot, in 1909, had been the first man to fly across the Channel, landing in a field behind Dover Castle. Though still dangerous and undertaken only by the intrepid few, the possibility of air travel caught the public imagination. For one man, however, the press tycoon Lord Northcliffe, there was also danger ahead: 'England is no longer an island … It means the aerial chariots of a foe descending on British soil if war comes.' Following this comment in 1906, Northcliffe was condemned as a scaremonger.

The south Kent towns of Dover and Folkestone had much in common: they were both seaside towns which, since the coming of the railways in the 1840s, had become the new playground of the middle and upper classes. They also had military links, with barracks and shooting ranges making a significant impact on the environment. The sight of men marching and the sound of gunfire were part of the character of the area. Historically, both towns were members of the Confederation of Cinque Ports, the ancient association of towns which came together at times of trouble to provide ships and men to defend the British coast from invaders.

Louis Blériot is saluted in Dover after his flight across the Channel in 1909.

Dover

In the town we have a comfortable prosperous-looking place, rich in story, but without any special features of interest to show.

The barracks, batteries and military works with which many parts of the heights about the town are covered and honey-combed need neither detain us nor move us to the contemptuous indignation of a Cobbett, but it is not possible to be long in or about Dover without being made aware that it is a garrison town.

The cliff which Edgar is supposed to have been describing [the writer is describing Shakespeare's Cliff as it featured in *King Lear*] has three practical interests attaching to it – through it runs a railway tunnel, and through it (when English people, as a gallant Admiral has twitted them, have thrown off fear) will be run the loop tunnel which will take trains down to the Channel Tube and so to France. Long talked about, often delayed, the 'Tunnel' seems an inevitable coming event as soon as timid opposition shall have been worn away. [Jerrold]

The visitor from Folkestone, arriving by road, enters near the Priory Station, from where an electric tram will bear him in a few minutes through the central part of the town to the sea-front or the Harbour Station, close to which is Admiralty Pier.

Along this the Continental boat trains run to and from the steamers. The pier owes its name to the fact that its construction was undertaken by the Lords of the Admiralty purely for naval purposes. The upper terrace is open to pedestrians and forms a delightful and very popular promenade. From the end of the pier the view extends westwards to Folkestone Pier, and north eastward along the white wall of chalk cliffs to the South Foreland.

The Admiralty Harbour. Here the largest warships may anchor beneath the protecting guns of the forts. The harbour cost three and a half millions, and was formally opened by the King, then the Prince of Wales, on October 15th 1909.

The Promenade Pier (Toll, 1d.; 2d. when band performs) is 900 feet long and 30 feet wide. At the end is a Pavilion accommodating 950 persons. At this pier the coast steamers for Deal, Ramsgate, Hastings, etc. land and embark their passengers. [Ward Lock Guide]

The South-Eastern & Chatham Railway owns a splendid fleet of nearly twenty steamers, some of them turbines, for its Dover and Folkestone crossings. The Continental and Indian mails go by Dover to Calais, but, though it is not generally known, the quickest journey from London to

Dover Harbour in peacetime.

Paris is that by Folkestone, which takes only six and three-quarter hours. [Mitton]

Dover must touch the heart of everyone who has any joy and pride in being born a Briton. The latest mode of Channel-crossing, however, needs no pier, and the aerodrome, about three miles inland, has already been the theatre for many a fine performance. Dover folk are getting so much used to seeing strange and gigantic birds hovering in the air, or gradually growing larger as they wing their way across the racing tides in the Channel, that they look at them with as much unconcern as most people do at motor-cars. [Mitton]

Postcard Home

March–past of Royal Artillery, King's birthday parade, Dover, 1909.

June 28th 1909

Dear Sarah Ann,

The weather today is dull but it held fine for the Birthday celebrations. This card does not do justice to it all, there were a lot more soldiers. I should think there were 3 or 400 in the bands alone. The Battleship the Terpsichore fired the first salute of large guns, followed by the midday gun and a volley of 7 guns, then all the troops fired and the bands played the King. This was all repeated again then all the troops shouted Hurrah 3 times for the King.

  Will

Folkestone

But the Camp – oh! The Camp. There was a fear that I should have three young 'soldiers' to bring home. Many an hour we spent watching the redcoats, bluecoats, whitecoats and anything that held a gun or a sword and to see the cavalry galloping to the tune of 'Bonnie Dundee' was the height of happiness. Many a rest we had in the gymnasium watching the drill or laughing at the clumsy attempts of some recruit to imitate his betters. (*The Holiday Annual* 1893)

It is a pleasant, prosperous seaside town so favoured by its situation, facing south and enringed by hills, that it has won repute as a mild health resort in our unpleasanter seasons and as a holiday place in summer time; its streets, its front and its Lees – or cliff walk – all bear witness at once to its popularity and to its prosperity, while down at the harbour with the coming and going of the Boulogne steamers, there is always matter to attract the lounging idler. [Jerrold]

At the Pleasure Gardens Theatre some of the best London companies perform throughout the year. The Victoria Pier, 680 feet in length, has a handsome Pavilion accommodating eight hundred persons. Here, or under the awning outside, concerts and band performances are given daily during the season.

  The Leas indisputably form one of the finest marine promenades in the world. A spacious carriage way, overlooked by terraces, crescents, and squares of dignified mansions, extends the whole distance, and between this and the cliffs are grassy walks along which a score of promenaders could walk arm in arm without discomfort, were any such vulgarity even thinkable at fashionable Folkestone.

  The Harbour. Since 1911 the steamers of the Flushing Royal Mail

Folkestone from the harbour. A particularly unusual postcard, as it was posted by a German soldier to his wife during the war. Perhaps he had been in Folkestone just before the war started.

Route have used the port of Folkestone for their night services. These speedy and magnificent cross channel vessels, with their luxurious state rooms and large number of double and single cabins, have made the route to Germany and beyond very popular. [Ward Lock Guide]

Folkestone falls from the cliff to the beach, as so many of these south coast towns do, and tired folk find the elevator railway very helpful. Steamers leave here for Boulogne – a very popular trip.

Between Folkestone and Dover the railway runs along beneath the towering cliffs which are associated in the minds of foreigners with England. There is just a ledge for the rails and the sea on the other side. From one of these terrible precipices near Dover it was once the fate of condemned malefactors to be hurled. [Mitton]

As the Victorian era made way for the twentieth century, Folkestone nosed ahead in the popularity stakes, and could claim to be Dover's glamorous sister. With its Leas, giving views across the Channel to the coast of France, and with extensive beaches and top-class hotels, it was the place to go for a seaside holiday. Dover had its disciples, but the beachfront was limited, and its aspect was confined to the harbour. The relationship between the two towns was one of healthy competition for holidaymakers and foreign travellers, and it is fair to say that Folkestone just had the edge. Certainly the foreign traveller had a more commodious journey from Folkestone.

The British Fleet off Folkestone just before the Great War.

Although both towns had a Harbour Station, that at Dover left the passenger with a lengthy walk along the pier to reach the ship's gangways, whereas Folkestone's station was on the harbour wall itself. Dover planned to overcome this disadvantage with its Marine Station, an architectural masterpiece, the building of which began in 1909. The spirit of competition

Glamorous Folkestone. These young ladies are being photographed on the Victoria Pier.

between the two ports would soon be forgotten and, instead, they would co-operate as never before, sharing many of the same experiences of wartime on Britain's front line.

Chapter 2
Folkestone 1914

The Great Adventure

Within days of the declaration of war, amidst much sabre-rattling and confidence born of a belief that the cause was just, the British Expeditionary Force was mobilized and sent to France to help cut off the German advance. Things began to unravel almost immediately. The retreat from Mons was hailed as a moral triumph, but an early German victory was prevented only by a determined counter-attack. French and British troops started to push the German army back until they reached the River Aisne. Here both sides seemed unable or unwilling to move any further. Although the German advance had been halted, all sides had suffered massive casualties. The British were least able to sustain such losses, having started the conflict with a relatively small standing army. This stalemate could not last for long:

The 3rd Hussars parade through Folkestone on 20 June 1914. Two months later they embarked for France with the BEF.

German reinforcements were heading for the front and it was clear that once they arrived the enemy would break out and advance on the coast. The Race to the Sea began, with the British slowly pushing into Belgium. Their objective was the ancient Flemish town which was to become the scene of so many battles, Ypres. Only fifteen miles from Calais, it had to be held at all costs. It was, but the cost was the practical annihilation of the BEF.

It was from Shorncliffe Camp, under the command of Brigadier Aylmer Haldane, that one element of the BEF, the 10th Infantry Brigade, set off for France in August 1914. Made up of the Royal Warwicks, the Royal Irish Fusiliers and the Seaforth Highlanders, the Brigade was accompanied by the 3rd (King's Own) Hussars.

The people of Folkestone had become used to the sound of the northern burr and Irish brogue and, in the evenings, the haunting sound of bagpipes drifted across the town. Just before the August Bank Holiday weekend of 1914 large crowds, families and friends, as well as local people, gathered at Shorncliffe for the annual inter-regimental sports day. Little did anyone know that, within a few days, the young men now doing battle on the sports field would be heading for France, and a battle from which many of them would not return. That summer was one of the finest for some years, and for the families who had flocked to the south coast for their holidays there was the additional treat of watching the soldiers marching confidently to the troopships to take them on to France. The Royal Navy warships patrolled just offshore, while overhead was the novel sight of aircraft gathering in formation to set off across the Channel. These were exciting times and few could then foresee the horrors ahead.

> The season was opening; thousands of visitors had flocked to the town [Folkestone], attracted by the health giving breezes from the sea and the charm of the scenery. Passengers crossing from the Continent watch for the white cliffs that stand for England.
>
> The charm of the Lower [Sandgate] Road is in danger of being marred by the stalls of the traders that dot the beach like rabbit hutches on the back garden. The steep cliffs and cable elevators remind one of Swiss scenery.
>
> Above there is the Leas, one of the finest promenades by the sea to be found in England, and one of the most popular health resorts in the world.
>
> Little did the happy throng of visitors dream that, just across the Channel, were all the preparations for a great War, that would outrage Belgium and lay waste to the fair fields of France.
>
> Many men joined the colours. The Folkestone Territorials were

invited to volunteer for service abroad, and quite a large percentage –
officers and men – readily responded to the call of the country. There
was no panic; no shrinking from duty; just a buzz of excitement, a
ripple of uncertainty, and an undercurrent of strength.

The band discoursed upon the Leas, but the gay crowd was not
there. The boys were enlisting; they were exchanging immaculate
collars and cuffs for the soldier's garb; women were asking what they
could do.

The town was the same, but life had changed from those old days.
The sportsmen no longer followed the hounds; they went to face the
Huns. Men looked over the sea with a touch of apprehension, and
before the end of the year the light of the moon was no longer a delight.
[Carlile]

Postcard Home
To: Miss Helen Taylor, Napanee, Ontario Canada

The Harbour, Folkestone.

3rd August 1914
Dear Helen,
I don't know when I'll get home as the War has started.
Jo

The Belgian Refugees

Carlile mentions the plight of Belgium. Despite her neutrality, Belgium was overrun by Germany as part of the Schlieffen Plan, which aimed to encircle French defences and take the invader all the way to the Channel coast. Britain had agreed to support Belgium in her neutrality, but the Kaiser did not believe that the British government would do so, at least not by taking up arms. There was outrage in Britain when Belgium was invaded, and the deployment of the BEF met with popular support. The Schlieffen Plan stalled and, as both sides

Belgian volunteers. This photograph accompanies Belgian military buttons and a note: 'A souvenir from our regiment at Folkestone to Mr Sidney Houghton. Long Live England.'

A Belgian Army recruitment form. Folkestone was the principal centre outside London for Belgians to enlist.

struggled to gain a few yards' advantage, the line along which the German advance was halted became known as the Western Front.

Within days of the outbreak of war, the people of Folkestone became the first in the country to witness some of the terrors of war. Arriving at the Harbour in fishing smacks, coalers and anything which could float, were Belgian refugees; they were tattered and torn, and worse. 'There were mothers who had been hounded from home and country before they could gather the little ones in their arms ... girls with flushed cheeks and wild terrified eyes whose stories others whispered under their breath. They were the victims of German lust.' [Carlile]

Over the next few weeks and months tens of thousands of refugees were provided for. Homes, medical treatment, food and work were provided and a newspaper, *Le Franco-Belge de Folkestone*, was established to help the refugees find missing relatives. Some who arrived were soldiers who had escaped capture or death in the face of the invading German army. Although they had been defeated, the resistance put up by the small Belgian army had been critical in disrupting the enemy advance. For the soldiers who escaped, Folkestone became the principal recruiting centre outside London to assist men to re-form and return to their homeland to take up the fight anew.

Despite the wretchedness of the vast majority of the refugees, the appearance of some caused good-natured smiles. A travelling acrobat arrived on one ship, together with his wife and the cannon from which he fired her into space. Many brought with them their treasured possessions, with bedding and sewing machines being high on the list, but also poultry and even parrots.

Most did not speak a word of English and their mother tongues were a mixture of Flemish and Walloon patois. Communication, though difficult, was never a real problem; the needs of most were obvious, and it was fortunate that the Belgian Vice-Consul in Folkestone, Adolph Petersen, was a Walloon speaker. Petersen was also a pastor and set up the Belgian Refugees' Committee at the Evangelical Church in Victoria Grove, from where he and his wife, Mary, co-ordinated the relief work.

Kitchener's Army

The ebb and flow of people to the Channel coast continued. The departure of the BEF in August 1914 was quickly followed by the arrival of the Belgian refugees. Then, to fill the gaps left by losses to the BEF, came the country's Territorial Battalions. But it was clear that more, many more, men would be needed if Britain was to stay in the fight. The call went out for volunteers and the first recruits to Kitchener's Army

Kitchener's Army. A recruitment rally at Marine Parade, Folkestone and recruits training at Shorncliffe.

began to arrive in south Kent. The Folkestone MP, Sir Phillip Sassoon, led the appeal locally with great success, especially from among the East Kent Yeomanry, with which he was serving. Men came forward in droves; the recruiting offices were unable to cope and, though few were turned away, the facilities for the new recruits were minimal. The new barracks at Shorncliffe could not accommodate all of the men. Huts and tents began to spring up on St Martin's Plain and at Dibgate. The *Folkestone Herald* of 16 October 1914 reported that wooden huts had been hastily erected in the grounds of the country mansion at Sandling by 350 workmen to house 8,000 men of Kitchener's Army. During the early days of the war, men from the Yorkshire and Lancashire Regiment and the Queen's Regiment were quartered at East and West Sandling camps. Even these camps could not take all of the men, and many were billeted in local hotels and homes. The home comforts provided by the landladies of Folkestone must have been welcome to the men after a hard day of training, for many of whom this was the first time away from home. After basic training in Aldershot, the men of the 8th Battalion of the Leicestershire Regiment arrived in Folkestone and were billeted in houses on the Leas and along Sandgate Road. The Leicester 'Tigers' were a typical example of the new army of lads eager to respond to the call to arms. Dick Read had been an engineering apprentice in Leicester before volunteering, and of his time in Folkestone before departing for the front he remembered '… long route marches in full equipment. Our Battalion became a reality, and I'm sure the survivors of the 110th Brigade will never forget the long and arduous ascents of the hill on the Dover Road, with the Valiant Sailor at the summit, and the Capel turn.'

Many had to make do with their own clothes, as uniforms were in short supply. Lack of rifles meant they had to use broomsticks for training. Occasionally the men had a glimpse of their eponymous leader:

In the early morning squads would march down to the Leas to begin the monotonous task of forming fours ... It was curious to see the fellows without a gun or even a walking stick going through the drill of lifting the rifle into position, sighting, and firing on command. Lord Kitchener, who had a residence at Broome Park, managed to come and go unobserved by the general public. K of K loved to mingle with the boys, watching their progress, nodding approval, and speaking words of counsel. Many a lad has amongst his most cherished memories a sentence from the lips of the great soldier. Great amusement was created by the bathing exercises. The boys came down to the beach in swarms, for a dip in the briny, or to roll in the surf. It was good to see the fellows in their fun capering about in the water. Large numbers of men were billeted all over the area. Town mansions, private hotels and cottages were packed with men. Praise of the men was heard on every side; poor people whose homes were filled with strange guests told how the boys often helped Mother wash-up and made their own beds; they played with the kiddies, and won the hearts of the girls. Soon after, in the terrible days in Flanders, they showed their quality in many a hard fight; but in their training they were soft hearted as boys at home. [Carlile]

Once their training was completed, albeit it to a standard which would have horrified the Old Contemptibles, the men were marched to Folkestone Harbour for the short trip across the Channel to Boulogne and on to the front line. The task of carrying the troops across the Channel fell principally to the pre-war cross-channel steamers which had plied between the ports of Folkestone and Dover and the French ports of Boulogne and Calais. These ships were commandeered by the Admiralty and redesignated His Majesty's Troop Ships, and as he sailed off to war, every man had his own fears and hopes. The following lines, the first verse of a poem by George Willis, provide a glimpse into Tommy Atkins' world.

What did I do, sonny, in the Great World War?
Well, I learned to peel potatoes and to scrub the barrack floor.
I learned to push a barrow and I learned to swing a pick,
I learned to turn my toes out, and to make my eyeballs click.

Highlanders land at Boulogne after their crossing from Folkestone.

I learned the road to Folkestone, and I watched the English shore,
Go down behind the skyline, as I thought, for evermore.
And the Blighty boats went by us and the harbour hove in sight,
And they landed us and sorted us and marched us 'by the right'.
'Quick march!' across the cobbles, by the kids who ran along
Singing 'Appoo?' 'Spearmant' 'Shokolah?' through dingy old
Boulogne;
By the widows and the nurses and the Blacks and Chinese,
And the gangs of smiling Fritzes, as saucy as you please.

Some 7,000 women of the WAACS also came to Folkestone for their training at the Metropole Hotel on the Leas, before they set sail for France to take up duties as drivers, mechanics and other jobs which would free the men to fight.

The volunteering spirit was widespread, but by no means universal. If 'doing your bit' was what every true Briton aspired to, 'shirking' was its antithesis. 'If there is one thing more than any other which exasperated the Territorial in the early days of the War it was reading in the newspapers about the Sanctity of the Season, "Business as Usual", and being made

Daddy, what did YOU do in the Great War?

One of the most powerful propaganda postcards of the war.

the subject of "Enthusiastic Scenes", these being composed largely of young men who ought to have been in our ranks, but who preferred to wear and wave flags.' So wrote Lieutenant Colonel A Atkinson, who commanded the local Territorial units of the East Kent Regiment, 'The Buffs'. This was a sentiment shared across the nation and led to the creation of the movement known as the 'White Feather Ladies', who would challenge men of apparent fighting age not in uniform and present them with the symbol of shame. Even Councillor John Jones of Folkestone was challenged on why he had not joined up, and he was over sixty.

Barely had the British army sailed for France in August 1914 than the first of the wounded began to arrive home. During the early days of the war, there developed something of a carnival atmosphere whenever a ship arrived at Folkestone. Such popular sentiment would not last; 1915 would bring home the stark reality of modern industrial warfare and the newspapers would feature the weekly lists of wounded, dead and missing.

The atmosphere of 1914 was captured in a late August edition of the *Folkestone Herald*: 'The first British wounded to be brought back to this country from the front were landed at Folkestone Harbour from Boulogne on Thursday and their arrival aroused great interest and excitement. The

La Guerre 1914-1915   Blessés anglais s'en allant de Boulogne à Folkestone.
195 R. P. **Paris**   English wounded returning from Boulogne to Folkestone.

Wounded soldiers returning from France to Folkestone.

soldiers were conveyed in motor cars through the town to the camp, being enthusiastically greeted by the crowds in the streets. Most of the men appeared to be slightly wounded and were able to walk with assistance. They displayed great cheerfulness.'

To cope with the ever-increasing number of casualties, the facilities of Shorncliffe Military Hospital and the Royal Victoria Hospital were bolstered by converting local hotels, convalescent homes and country houses into hospitals. Beechborough House was immediately made available, opening in October 1914 with fifty-five beds for the treatment of wounded Belgian soldiers and then British troops as more and more wounded came back from France. Other hospitals were set up at St Andrew's Convalescent Home on the East Cliff, at York House, originally a nursing home, at Manor House, once the home of the Earl of Radnor, and at the Bevan in Sandgate, another former convalescent home. Volunteers from the local Red Cross and St John Ambulance Brigade made up the men and women of the Volunteer Aid Detachments. VAD Kent 9, of the local St John Ambulance Brigade, set up shop in 1914 at Folkestone Harbour to provide immediate care to the thousands of Belgian refugees and soldiers. Many of the patients were nursed by female volunteers, while the manual task of getting the wounded to the hospitals fell to their male counterparts. Before the Folkestone Warren landslip at the end of 1915, the wounded soldiers were either brought by ship direct to Folkestone, or they were landed at Dover and taken there by train.

Wounded British soldiers began to arrive in considerable numbers at the end of 1914, for treatment in local hospitals. The method of working was for telephonic messages to be sent from the Military Hospitals to Mr Evans and Mr Jones (Commandant of St John Ambulance Brigade and Chief Fire Officer of Folkestone, respectively), stating the probable time of arrival of the train, and giving the number of stretcher and walking cases.

Stretchers were prepared on the platform, and the men stood by until the train arrived, which often meant waiting several hours. On the coming of the wounded, walking cases were taken in cars, lent by residents, and by motor char-a-bancs, while the cot cases, on stretchers, were placed in the ambulance wagons. One hundred and twenty one hospital trains, with 12,300 wounded, were tended by the VAD men. [Carlile]

The training and resilience of these volunteers was severely tested within weeks of the outbreak of war. On the night of 26 October 1914 the *Amiral Ganteaume*, a French steamer with 2,200 French and Belgian refugees aboard, was sailing from Calais to Le Havre when she was struck by either a mine or a torpedo. The *Queen*, a troopship returning empty from Boulogne, answered the distress flares but found she could not launch her boats because of a heavy sea. Despite the risk of mines and any lurking enemy

SS Queen *in her pre-war role as a cross-channel steamer.*

submarines, Captain Carey manoeuvred alongside the stricken vessel and
kept station until all of the passengers had jumped or been manhandled
across to the *Queen*. The rescue operation was witnessed by a journalist from
the *Daily Chronicle* who was on board the *Queen*:

> The side of The Queen touched the sinking ship. The refugees leapt at
> us by the score. We helped them aboard. The Red Cross men and an
> officer and I cleared a path to the companionway to get them below to
> make room for the mass that pressed on. Some were so fear stricken
> that they had to be led to the companionway. Others, those who had
> been in the trenches, were quiet, and helped to clear the decks. Mothers
> tossed their babies to us, and were pulled over themselves. Some were
> jambed [sic] between the heaving ships. Others, half dressed for
> swimming, took flying leaps at us. The last of the Belgians was got
> aboard. He was a soldier of the 8th regiment of the Line. The news –
> unfortunately not true – flashed round that all were saved. There never
> was a louder cheer. Vive l'Angleterre!

With her additional cargo, many of whom were wounded, the *Queen* made
for Folkestone and, as she steamed into her berth, a great cheer went up
from the packed decks. All through the night, the refugees were brought to

*Rounded up. Germans arrested in Folkestone being marched from the harbour to
Shorncliffe Camp and internment.*

shore by the volunteers. Some of the men had untreated wounds from the battlefield and all were tired, hungry and dishevelled. Food and hot drinks were awaiting them all and those needing urgent medical attention were despatched to one of the many hotels and hospitals brought into service that night.

Aliens, Spies and DORA

Folkestone and its inhabitants quickly developed a curiously marked dual personality. We have seen the way that soldiers and refugees in their thousands were welcomed to the town. But there was a more sinister side and this became evident very soon after the declaration of war. Encouraged by a prolific government poster campaign warning of spies, cautioning against loose talk and vilifying anything that smacked of being German, Folkestonians took these messages to heart. The Reverend Carlile described the scenes:

> There were many German and Austrian residents; scarcely one of the hotels or larger pensions was without Germans on the staff. Within a few days 285 German reservists arrived at the harbour to join the Kaiser's forces. They were detained and an escort was sent down from the camp [Shorncliffe], and the prisoners were marched along Sandgate Road, and finally sent to very comfortable quarters at Horsham. Within days Folkestone was made a prohibited area. All aliens were required to register and satisfy the Chief Constable as to their reasons for wishing to remain in the town. During the first week more than 1,000 aliens applied for permits.

Any foreign national who did not register could find himself in serious trouble. Two Austrian men, both local waiters before the war, found themselves in Folkestone Police Court in August 1914, charged with being enemy aliens and having failed to register. Their defence that there were many others who had not done so cut very little ice with the court and both were sentenced to three months in prison with hard labour. In the same court two German ladies were also called to account. They said that they believed the requirement to register only applied to men and, in any event, they were not enemies. They were luckier than the men, being fined £2. 6d.

Barely a week passed during the early months of the war without a report in the local papers of someone falling foul of the registration requirements. The government poster campaign was underpinned by the Defence of the Realm Act (better known simply as DORA), which gave swingeing powers to both civil and military authorities. Part of Folkestone was designated a

Restricted Area, owing to the presence of so many troops, whose safety was paramount. There was constant worry about the presence of spies, who might have gleaned valuable information and then tried to board a channel steamer (there was still a reduced service for civilian travellers), to take their information back to Berlin. 'Spy Mania' took a firm hold in the town. Councillor John Jones gives an insight into the phenomenon, with people perhaps settling old scores by making malicious reports. Then there were the genuine but invariably mistaken reports: 'I had just gone to bed one night when a knock came to the door. We were invited to go and look at a house at the back where, it was said, someone was signalling. A lady was sure it was because her daughter, who was at the Post Office, understood Morse Code. We all gathered round and concentrated our attention on the window. It was discovered that the so-called signal was caused by the erratic wind blowing through a broken window.'

To enforce the multitude of regulations, an army of special constables was recruited. While there is no doubt that many performed valuable service, some who were attracted to this work were little more than trouble-making busybodies. John Jones had little time for pompous officialdom and does not spare his townsmen in his criticisms, including the Chief Constable of Folkestone Borough police, Mr Harry Reeve – despite the fact that they were next-door neighbours. The growing contingent of special constables comes in for special mention: 'Many ludicrous situations arose. I recollect one beautiful moonlit night, one of my friends, a great Trade Unionist, called and in a most autocratic manner ordered me to "Put that light out!" – he had been appointed a Special Constable and he was going to carry out his duty. As a matter of fact the gas was turned off. Eventually he discovered it was the old "parish lamp" – the light of the moon reflected from a piece of plate glass mirror I had in my window to extend the vision of the apples and oranges when short of stock. He went off disgusted!'

An early casualty of Spy Mania was the humble pigeon. These were the days before wireless, and the value of the homing carrier pigeon was quickly identified. Within days of the outbreak of war the Folkestone and District Homing Pigeon Society had offered its birds to the Secretary of State for War. But this messenger of war could fly in both directions and suspicion soon fell on the poor creature. DORA outlawed the keeping of carrier pigeons without a licence and Folkestone's Chief Constable issued an order that if any illegally kept pigeons were found in the town they would be released without notice. Such a threat was the poor bird thought to be that some advocated a 'shoot on sight' policy. Their plight was raised in *The Scotsman*: 'Already all over the country numbers of birds, the property of innocent owners, have been shot. So serious has the menace become that the National Homing Union have issued a warning to the general public that the shooting of homing pigeons is illegal.'

Ironically, unknown to the spy-obsessed people of Folkestone, the town actually was a hotbed of espionage. Military Intelligence, the forerunner of today's MI5, was quick to realize that some of the refugees arriving at the harbour might have valuable information about events in Europe. Some might even be persuaded to return to gather more. Under the control of Colonel George Kynaston Cockerill, Folkestone became the headquarters of a tripartite bureau, including French and Belgian intelligence officers. The British section was based in Marine Parade, Folkestone, and was headed by Captain (later Major) Cecil Aylmer Cameron, whose codename was 'Evelyn', but who was usually referred to as 'B', to distinguish him from the London chief, 'C'.

As soon as Louise de Bettignies arrived at Folkestone in October 1914 it was clear to the officers at the refugee centre that she was special, and her details were quickly passed to Major Cameron. Louise was found accommodation in a local hotel and that evening she received a visit from Cameron. He established that Louise was thirty-four years of age and came

Spies in Folkestone. Louise de Bettignies and Mata Hari.

from a noble French family. She was well travelled and confident and, when asked if she would be willing to train as an agent, she readily agreed. She was fluent not only in French but also in Italian and German. The training began and the techniques taught were surprisingly sophisticated. These included writing in invisible ink on tissue paper, and messages in the hems of skirts and engraved in minute letters on the lenses of spectacles.

Louise was given the operational name of Alice Dubois and she set off for France to establish a new network of spies and to organize escape routes for Allied prisoners. These were the days before radio, and messages were sent back to Folkestone by homing pigeons. The 'Dubois Service', as it became known, provided critical information which led to the destruction of several German batteries and, most notably, provided details of the date and time when the Kaiser's train would be visiting Lille. Several bombers were despatched to attack the train and it was only by chance that none of the bombs hit the German Emperor's carriage.

In October 1915 Louise was given instructions by Major Cameron to travel to Tournai and then to Brussels to organize the agents there. By this time the Germans had become much more alert to the presence of spies. It was the week before Louise set off on her latest mission that Edith Cavell had been caught and executed by firing squad. Louise was carrying her instructions on a thin roll of paper wrapped inside her signet ring. When she was stopped for an identity check, it soon became clear that it would be more than a cursory examination. Louise removed the roll of paper and tried to swallow it, but her actions were noticed by the German officer. She was arrested, convicted and sentenced to death. The sentence was later commuted to life in prison, and Louise de Bettignies contracted tuberculosis as a result of the appalling conditions in which she was held. She died on 17 September 1918. She may have found some comfort in learning that the Allies had retaken Ostend and Lille.

Another woman who passed through the hands of Military Intelligence in Folkestone was Margaretha Geertruida Zelle. She was picked up at Folkestone Harbour in December 1915, waiting to embark on a boat for France. Secret reports reveal that she was questioned by Captain S Dillon, who noted: 'Although she had good answers to every question, she impressed me very unfavourably, but after having her very carefully searched and finding nothing, I considered I hadn't enough grounds to refuse her embarkation. She was handsome, bold … well and fashionably dressed [in a costume with] raccoon fur trimming and hat to match.' The woman told Dillon that she was travelling to The Hague to be with her lover, a Dutch colonel. A later report disclosed that she was 'in relation with highly placed

Léon Trulin. One of the youngest spies, recruited in Folkestone. The post against which he stood when executed in Lille.

people and during her sojourn in France she made the acquaintance of many French and Belgian officers. She is suspected of having been to France on an important mission for the Germans.' In pre-war Paris Zelle had acquired a reputation as an exotic dancer and courtesan, and she was better known as Mata Hari. Her confidence and ability to talk her way out of trouble deserted her in 1917 when she was arrested in France. The secret report states that she confessed to the French: 'Mata Hari today confessed that she has been engaged by Consul Cremer of Amsterdam for the German Secret Service.' In fact, later information about her trial revealed that Mata Hari strenuously denied her guilt. Tried and convicted by a court martial, Mata Hari was executed by firing squad. The story of her activities as a spy is still one of the most enduring of the Great War. How different it might have been if Major Dillon had found something incriminating on her that day in Folkestone.

Léon Trulin was seventeen and lived with his mother and nine sisters in Lille when the Germans invaded Belgium. He wanted to fight for his country and in May 1915 he stole away, making his way into Holland and then finding a boat to England. He arrived at Folkestone where he found his way to Adolph Petersen, whom he asked to help him join the Belgian army. The boy failed the medical assessment, but jumped at the chance of becoming a secret agent and, following a week's training at Folkestone's spy school in unit and artillery recognition, he was slipped back into Belgium. His task done, the young spy returned to Folkestone on 26 July 1915 to present his report and, such was the quality of his information, that he was then introduced to the British spymaster, Cameron. His next mission was to return to enemy territory and to recruit local agents to set up observation on the railway network.

When another agent was arrested, Léon realized that he was in danger of being discovered, so he made for the Dutch border. He was caught trying to burrow under the electrified fence on the Belgian–Dutch border and, at his trial, was sentenced to death by firing squad. As he awaited his execution, Léon Trulin wrote a deeply moving last letter to his mother with strict instructions that it be delivered after 10 am. Leon had just turned eighteen years of age.

'It will be over by Christmas'

Despite early predictions, the war did not finish by Christmas. The famous winter truce of 1914, when British and German troops climbed out of their trenches and exchanged gifts, was the last time any goodwill would be shown – the generals saw to that. Both sides dug in along what became known as the Western Front and the men did their best to cope with the mud and misery of trench life.

Christmas 1914. Recruits enjoying the festivities at Shorncliffe Camp.

Christmas in Folkestone was enjoyed to the full, with soldiers, residents and visitors able to choose from a full programme of seasonal entertainments. As well as a choice of cinemas, there was live entertainment at the Pleasure Gardens Theatre, where the Vaudeville production of *My Aunt* received positive reviews. There was great anticipation with Bernard Shaw's new play *Pygmalion* due to open just after Christmas. The Leas Shelter was always popular, providing live music every evening, without charging any entrance fee. Had it not been for the fact that so many in the audiences were wearing khaki, one could have doubted that there really was a war on. But, yes, there was a war on, and one Folkestone resident perhaps spoke for many when recalling: 'My parents used to dread opening the daily papers and reading the names of the hundreds of casualties of the war. We children used to watch the soldiers marching down the slope from the Leas to the harbour to board the troop ships to take them to France. At first, they all came down singing as they marched, songs like "Pack up Your Troubles", "Take Me Home to Blighty", "Keep the Home Fires Burning", etc. Later, as the war went on, there was only the sound of their marching feet.'

Chapter 3
Folkestone 1915–1918

The Arrival of the Canadians

In a remarkable response to Britain's call to arms, the sons and daughters of her Empire volunteered in their hundreds of thousands. From Canada, the land of the maple leaf, the First Contingent of 30,000 men arrived at Salisbury Plain in the autumn of 1914. These men were led by General R A H Alderson, who had served previously in the Royal West Kents. The men had a miserable time at Salisbury, heavy rains causing flooding and fields of mud.

Even as the First Contingent was arriving in England, the recruitment campaign in Canada was under way for the Second, then the Third and Fourth, Contingents. 'Canada came to Shorncliffe in force in February, 1915, and very soon Folkestone was a suburb of Toronto; within the year 40,000 men were in training.' With these words the Reverend J C Carlile sums up what was, perhaps, the most significant change to Folkestone during the Great War. During the remainder of the war many thousands of Canadians came to the Kent coast. They lived in huts and tents at Shorncliffe, Dibgate, St Martin's Plain, Sandling and Otterpool. As these men went off to fight, some sustained wounds and injuries and, in due course, they might well find themselves in one of the many hospitals set up throughout Kent to look after them.

The men had some basic training at camps in Canada, but the real work was done while in England. On the hills around Folkestone had been dug a system of trenches as a precaution against invasion. These, supplemented by additional practice trenches, enabled the men to practise the skills needed at the front, including 'going over the top'. Then there was grenade throwing and bayonet practice and, of course, route marches. Opinion seems to have been divided on the value of these exercises. Private Donald Fraser wrote in his Journal:

> Friday September 17 1915: After four months training in Kent, England, where we had a very enjoyable time, first at Dibgate in the vicinity of Shorncliffe, then at Lydd where we had a rush shooting

Canadian soldiers on a route march from their camp at Sandling, near Folkestone.

practice … we were considered fit and skilled in the art of warfare, ready to meet the hated Hun. When I think of it, our training was decidedly amateurish and impractical. It consisted mainly of route marches and alignment movements. Our musketry course amounted to nothing; we had only half an idea about the handling of bombs. We were perfectly ignorant regarding rifle grenades.

In contrast, Captain J W Margeson of the 25th Infantry Battalion (Nova Scotia) wrote home to his local newspaper on 9 September 1915:

East Sandling. Our camp is beautifully situated, sheltered between the hills in the County of Kent. In this valley about 75,000 Canadian boys are in training. All the men have had their practice at the Hythe shooting ranges, which are looked upon as the finest in the world. Trench warfare has been undertaken and it would surprise you to see how quickly the 25th Battalion can 'dig themselves in' and prepare to meet the foe. Much more has been accomplished which I am not privileged at this time to make known. However, you can take it from me that the boys are ready – prepared to fight, prepared to die if necessary for the preservation of those liberties which Canadians have enjoyed across the seas.

With the arrival of the Second Contingent fresh from Canada, the remnants of the First Contingent were transferred from Tidworth Camp to

The CANADIANS are "holding their own" at Shorncliffe

The Canadians were popular with the locals!

Shorncliffe, including the Canadian Army Medical Corps. As the war years passed, the medical facilities in Folkestone became stretched and more facilities were added. Shorncliffe Military Hospital became No. 9 Canadian Stationary Hospital, and annexes were formed at Beechborough House (renamed Queen's Canadian Hospital) and the Bevan in Sandgate. Westcliffe Hotel (renamed West-cliffe Canadian Eye & Ear Hospital), close to Holy Trinity church, was also taken over and took on the pioneering role of treating facial injuries by plastic surgery. Many other hotels and convalescent homes were converted to medical use.

The Reverend Carlile gives us some clues about how the Canadians were regarded by the local inhabitants: 'Hundreds of boys on Sunday afternoons were guests in Folkestone homes, and were more than welcome. They endeared themselves to the children, and captured the hearts of the girls so successfully that about 1,100 Canadian brides went from the district to strengthen the tie of the Empire across the seas.'

There was, however, a darker side to encounters between troops and local girls. As a garrison town, Folkestone had always had its complement of 'camp followers' and, at the outbreak of war, a number of girls had been literally rounded up from what John Jones called their 'Abodes of Love' and told to leave town. This draconian measure did not cure the problem and it became necessary to turn the old TB sanatorium hospital at Etchinghill, just outside town, into a hospital to treat the men who succumbed to temptation and contracted venereal diseases. Jones made no reference to this problem when giving his own light-hearted description:

> Canadian heroes and British warriors, especially the junior section, looked with a merry eye upon the feminine heroines of Folkestone. Like the busmen of old, they adopted the motto, 'None but the brave deserve the fair,' and the fair reciprocated as only British damsels will. The gay promenades were visited very frequently, but secluded spots were also selected: Lovers' Walks, Madeira Walk, the Sea-Shore where they could breathe sweet nothings in each other's ears to the roar of the sea shells and to the ripple of the waves, and, while winning the War, these certain sections of Folkestone were happy. But alas! In war times, as in peace times, happiness is not always permanent. The course of love, whether true or illicit has its obstacles. The terrible Mrs Grundy arrived and other forbidding personages of the Social Purity League.

One thing is certain: for young men so far from home, who knew only too well that their futures could be reckoned in days rather than years, the prospect of a smile, a kiss, perhaps more, from a Folkestone lass did more for morale than a rousing speech from any number of generals. In July 1915 Private Charlie Thicke was stationed at Risborough Barracks and, as he waited to be sent to the front, he wrote to his parents in Canada:

> Dear Mother and Father, Well, I am in England, and only twenty miles from France, but even so, I shall not be satisfied until I get there and see a bit of the fun, and get back. That will be a happy day. Oh! By the way, I intend to send my ring home. If I do not some German will take it from me – if he can. Say, if I come back with a little Belgium girl don't be surprised, for they are a pretty lot and this place – Folkestone – has lots of them. Mother, dear, fry me two eggs, and prepare toast and coffee. Goodbye. Love and kisses to all. Charlie.

Even when at the front, thoughts of female company were never far away. Private Jack Branch of the 28th (North West) Battalion was a member of a wiring party in No Man's Land when he took a shrapnel bullet through his arm. Although in great pain, he soon realized that the injury was not going to permanently disable him, but was bad enough to warrant his medical evacuation to England and, as he was carried out of the line by the stretcher-bearers, he cheerfully called to the rest of his platoon, 'I'll give your love to all the girls at Shorncliffe.'

When the Canadians wrote home they would often give their impressions of the people and countryside of south Kent. The following letter was written from West Sandling Camp by an unknown soldier in the 20th Infantry Battalion (1st Central Ontario Regiment) to his wife in Canada. It demonstrates the anxiety felt by men so far from home if they did not hear from their loved ones. Also of interest is the description of Hythe and Folkestone, and some of the machinery of war which had arrived in the area.

Dear Mabel, I think it is about time I am dropping you a few lines to let you know I am still in the land of the living. I have been looking forward to a few lines from you but I expect you have been busy. As you know we are stationed near Shorncliffe. There are only a few towns near here that we can go to, the rest being out of bounds. Hythe is one of the nearest. It is right on the seashore and they have quite a bathing beach. It is like all the other towns near here, all being very old fashioned. The streets are about as straight as a cat's hind leg and resemble a cow path more than anything else. The streets are just wide enough for two autos to pass and no more. The sidewalks are just wide enough for two. If you meet anyone it is almost a case of taking to the road. There are innumerable little alleys and lanes just about wide enough for a buggy to go through.

Folkestone is just such another place as Hythe only it is a little bigger and more busy but that isn't saying much for either just now. Both towns are seaside resorts and that business is just about dead. I don't know what they would do without our boys as they leave a lot of money. You can't go to either town without seeing them every way that you look, and in big crowds too.

Aeroplanes are very common around here, some go over the camp every day. One Sunday there were somewhere in the neighbourhood of sixty went over. There is a big Airship around quite a bit too. We call it the Silver Queen and it looks just like silver. One of the boys got a dandy snapshot of it. It comes down very low sometimes so we can get a good look at it.

We can see boats of all kinds on the sea from here and it is a wonder that the German subs don't sink more. There was one captured by one of our destroyers near to Folkestone a few days ago. The boys say that in one of the harbours near, Dover, there are 42 German subs that have been captured, of course that is kept quiet. They have steel nets and traps that extend from Folkestone over to France and only one opening and that is guarded by ships. Write soon to Hub.

Clarence Booth: the Soldier's Tale

Many Canadians were young men who had been born in Britain but had emigrated over the last decade or so to seek their fortunes in a young country. Clarence Booth was such a man. Clarrie grew up in Hythe and emigrated to Canada in 1912 to work on the Canadian Pacific Railroad, but found that he preferred tending a hardware store in Edmonton. He volunteered in January 1915 and, following basic training in Canada embarked aboard the SS *Metagama* at Montreal and set sail for England, eventually arriving at Shorncliffe Camp in Folkestone on 30 September. Private Booth was assigned to the 49th (Edmonton) Battalion Canadian Infantry, part of the Canadian 3rd Division. Clarrie was back home and proudly visited friends and family in his new khaki uniform with the brightly polished maple leaf badge on his cap.

The 49th Battalion marched from Shorncliffe to Folkestone Harbour on 9 October and boarded the troopships for Boulogne. No sooner had Private Booth landed in France than he was given a pick, something against which anyone who knew Clarrie would have urged caution. The predictable result was that he sustained an injured hand and had to report to the Field Ambulance for treatment. After a swift recovery he was able to rejoin his unit. The 3rd Division saw little action over the next few months but, in spring 1916, the three Canadian Divisions were sent forward to relieve the British troops to the east of Ypres. The British had battled for nearly two years to keep the high ground of Mount Sorrel and Tor Top (also known as Hill 62), but as spring moved into summer, the sector seemed quiet. Unknown to the Allies, the Germans had spent six weeks preparing an attack on the two summits: mines had been laid and additional artillery had been brought forward. At dawn on 2 June, after a devastating artillery barrage, the German XIII Corps attacked. The Canadians suffered heavy casualties but, despite desperately fighting to retain their ground, they were forced to concede Mount Sorrel and Tor Top. Reserves were brought forward and a counter-attack was planned for the next day. The 7th Canadian Brigade was called forward, and this included Private Booth in the 49th Battalion. The signal to attack was due to be given at 6 am, but confusion arose when six signal rockets were prematurely ignited. What should have been three simultaneous attacks became piecemeal and the Germans were able to concentrate their fire on each front in turn. Although the Canadians were able to close some gaps in the line, by early afternoon they had to fall back to their start positions.

During the fierce fighting, some of it hand to hand, Private Booth was shot – a bullet or shrapnel caught his right shoulder, smashing his collar

EXAMINATION
BY
STANDING MEDICAL BOARD, SHORNCLIFFE.

aug 7th 1916.

No. _436419_ Unit _49th Batt 9th Res._ Rank _Pte_

Name _Booth C D_ Age _23_

Examination held at _C C a C_

DISABILITY.

Overseas—Imperial
(scratch one out) _G.S.W at shoulder (June 3/16 Ypres)_

Present Condition: _4th Frame 9 mo—_

Wounded in right shoulder by shrapnel fracturing Clavicle at inter third. Wound healed. Fracture united – long callus – at site of fracture : and Under-crowd will carry a part

Board recommends :

1. Fit for Duty.
2. Fit for duty after_____weeks physical training.
3. Fit for light duty_____weeks.
4. Fit for Permanent Base Duty.
5. Discharge.

Signatures :

_____ Pres.

Members _____

Approved.

Shorncliffe _aug 7_ 1916. _____ Capt.
for A.D.M.S.
Canadian Training Division.

A medical certificate issued at Shorncliffe confirming Clarrie Booth's gunshot wound.

bone. He managed to return to his lines and was evacuated to the No. 1 Canadian Military Hospital at Étaples and from there back to Blighty. Meanwhile, the depleted Canadian battalions continued to fight for Mount Sorrel, culminating in an assault by two composite battalions on 13 June. Under cover of a smokescreen the men moved forward and succeeded in dislodging the Germans. Over the past two weeks the Canadians had lost 8,430 officers and men, killed missing or wounded, but they had regained their pride and acquired a reputation for tenacity and hard fighting.

Back in England Clarrie was sent for convalescence, followed by two weeks' home leave in Cheriton, where the Booth family now lived at the Oddfellows Club in Broomfield Road. Where and when they had met is not known but the dashing young soldier had caught the eye of a young lady of twenty-five from Oxfordshire. Lilias May White was living on the King's Road in Chelsea in 1916 when she met Clarrie and they fell in love. A quiet wedding at Christ Church in Chelsea was followed by a honeymoon in Ramsgate, but then came separation as the soldier returned to barracks and Lilias to London. In June 1917, Clarrie arrived at Bramshott Camp near Aldershot and was posted to the 21st Reserve Battalion, where his football skills were noticed – he was picked to play for the battalion team and travelled the country playing matches. The competitions were good for morale and a large turnout was always assured. For Clarrie and his team

The Canadian 21st Battalion Reserve football team. Clarrie is in the back row on the right.

there were successes; they took the Northern Command title, beating the 1st Battalion Machine Gun Corps by 6 goals to 2 at the Elland Road ground of Leeds United. In 1918 came the supreme prize when the 21st Reserve

Clarrie was also an entertainer. He is seen here in the back row on the left.

Clarrie and Lilias Booth with their daughter, Edna.

Battalion won the title of champions of the Canadian Military Forces (British Isles). The final was played at Seaford against the 11th Reserve Battalion, based at Shorncliffe. The Bramshott team took a three-goal lead in the first half from which, despite a fight-back in the second, the Shorncliffe men were unable to recover. Clarrie and his team-mates were each presented with a gold winner's medal and the silver Championship trophy. Clarrie was also part of a troupe of soldiers known as the Follies. Providing musical and comic entertainment, the men toured the Canadian camps helping to maintain the morale of the troops.

On 6 June 1919 Private Booth was discharged from the army, and he and Lilias and their daughter, Edna, lived for a year in Wandsworth before moving to Folkestone and setting up home in Chart Road. They lived out their lives happily in Folkestone, with two more children, Clarence (always known as Eric) and Dennis. Clarrie continued to play football and also acquired a local reputation as a whist player. During the Second World War he joined the Post Office Home Guard detachment. Lilias died in 1969, with Clarence following in 1973, never having returned to Canada.

To the Western Front

As their training came to an end, the Canadian Second Contingent prepared to depart for the front. On 2 September 1915 they were paraded at Beechborough for an inspection by the King. He had a message for them: 'The past weeks at Shorncliffe have been for you a period of severe and rigorous training ... History will never forget the loyalty and readiness with

The King rides through Cheriton in 1915 after inspecting the Canadians.

which you rallied to the aid of your Mother Country in the hour of danger. My thoughts will be with you. May God bless you and bring you victory.'

Within days the Canadian Second Contingent began to follow in the footsteps of Kitchener's Army: a march along the Leas, down Slope Road to the harbour and a troopship to Boulogne. The journey from the peaceful Kent countryside to the mayhem of the front took a matter of hours. Even before they had left English soil, the soldiers could hear the ominous rumble of war drifting across the Channel, as reported by Lieutenant S C Kirkland, who was camped at West Sandling: 'When there is a heavy bombardment on around Zeebrugge or at the west of the battle line at Dunkirk, or in the direction of Ypres, we can distinctly hear the rumble of the big guns ... I thought at first the noise I heard was thunder but as I was hearing it every morning I made enquiries and was told it was the noise of battle.'

The journey from Folkestone to Boulogne usually went off without a hitch; sometimes there was a delay if a new minefield in the Channel had to be cleared or if enemy submarines had been spotted. Apart from that the worst part of the crossing was likely to be a touch of seasickness. On the other hand the 28th (North West) Battalion experienced an embarrassing debacle when, in September 1915, they set off for Folkestone Harbour.

From Private Donald Fraser, whose views on the adequacy of the training have already been noted, we have a graphic description:

Friday, September 17, 1915: Anyway, our training was at an end, word was passed around that we were leaving today for France. The camp was all excitement. At last we were to witness real fighting. It was almost too good to be true. Everyone was pleased at the idea though a bit dubious of the outcome. The consequences, however, were thrown to the winds, the only thing that mattered was we were bound for France. Orders to strike camp were given and in due time we were on the move, our packs choke full of clothing, etc. It was a memorable day as our brigade stepped out on the road and marched for Folkestone through Lympne, Hythe, Seabrook and Sandgate. The march was a gruelling one. Our packs were so heavy that the strappings almost cut into the flesh and there were many connivances employed to ease the aching back, and shoulders. Near Folkestone at the Leas we halted and lay on the road. By this time the stragglers had caught up. It soon became evident that there was something wrong and everyone was enquiring the reason for the delay. The command rang out along the lines, 'About turn!', then we learned the reason – there were mines in the English Channel and we could not cross until the sweepers announced all clear. Our first battle, the retreat from Folkestone, commenced. Twos and threes were falling out by the roadside, the climb to the plains above Sandgate took the heart out of many, so they took up their abode for the night on the roadside, in gardens, in the fields, amidst bushes, and a few fortunate ones managed to get into houses. The Companies got badly mixed. By the time a halt was called the battalion was widely scattered. About a couple of dozen, including the writer, represented 'A' Company. That night we slept on [Sir John Moore's] Plains under the canopy of heaven with only what we carried with us for covering. Next morning and forenoon the stragglers began to arrive from all directions and by the afternoon we were up to strength again ...

Saturday, September 18, 1915: The channel was evidently clear for in the early evening we were on the road again. At Folkestone we embarked. The British Navy had its sentinels out, one particular vessel keeping a watchful eye on us. It darted hither and thither, racing alongside us or crossing our bow or stern. In the fading light England was soon lost to view – to many forever.

For those Canadians in camp on the night of 13 October 1915, the thunder of war came much closer. That night five German Zeppelins carried out an attack on London and the home counties. Kapitänleutnant Alois Böcker, commanding L14, turned south and headed for Otterpool Camp at Lympne. The official records of the 2nd Canadian Division

HM Troopship Victoria *at Folkestone Harbour, laden with men en route to France.*

describe what happened:

> The camps of Otterpool and Westenhanger were visited by a Zeppelin while occupied by the 5th, 6th, and 7th Artillery Brigades of the 2nd Division. It was later on in the year, after the division had removed from the area with the exception of these three units. 'Lights Out' had just been sounded when the humming of the Zeppelin engines announced its approach. Almost at once, and before it could be realized that a raid was intended, five bombs were dropped in rapid succession, exploding with terrific force in an oblique line across the camp of Otterpool. The first landed in a hedge bordering the field, the second struck the guard tent squarely, the third fell in the men's lines, and the fourth in the horse lines, the fifth striking a temporary road and exploding without damage. The Zeppelin then crossed the road and straightening its course parallel to Westenhanger Camp dropped five more bombs. Luckily the exact position of the lines was fifty yards to the left, and this error in judgment on the part of the navigator of the Zeppelin undoubtedly saved many lives, for the bombs exploded harmlessly in the race-track enclosure. At Otterpool, however, there were considerable casualties among men and horses. It was presumed

at the time of the raid that the Zeppelin in making its way towards London had drifted too far south and was returning to its base when the camp was sighted, although the position of the two camps in relation to one another seemed to be fairly accurately known.

Fifteen men were killed and twenty-one injured in the raid.

E. S. 193. Boulogne-sur-Mer
Publicité locale Hors Concours
(Reproduction interdite)

Stevenard, edit., Boulogne-sur-Mer

Postcard Home

Active Service – 22-3-15
To: Mrs A D Murphy, 56 Dover St, Folkestone
My dear Chippy, Isn't this a nice card.
    Fondest love from Alf

'Boulogne undies'.

The Troopships

Although the Canadians had taken up permanent residence in Folkestone, they were by no means the only troops to come to the town. As the war progressed, there arrived a steady flow of men on their way to France. Initially, they were found temporary accommodation within the existing army barracks and camps, but these were far from ideal, with inadequate facilities and being some distance from Folkestone Harbour, an

Date (1915)	Unit	Notes
4 July	12th Btn Highland Light Infantry	814 men plus officers
10 July	10th Btn Worcester Regiment	Part of the 19th Division
10 July	7th Btn KOSB	
? July	7th Btn The Buffs (East Kent) Regiment	
15 July	12th (Service) Btn Manchester Regiment	
18 July	5th Btn Canadian Infantry (Saskatchewan)	
25 July	8th (Service) Btn Norfolk Regiment	997 men and 34 officers
26 July	7th Btn Bedfordshire Regiment	820 men and 31 officers
27 July	8th Btn East Surrey Regiment	Part of 55th Infantry Brigade
27 July	7th (Service) Btn The Queen's Regiment	Part of 55th Infantry Brigade
29 July	7th Btn Leicester Regiment	Part of 110th Brigade
31 July	8th (Service) Btn East Lancashire Regiment	
31 July	5th Canadian Siege Battery	After training at Lydd

inconvenience if the scheduled crossing was delayed or cancelled. Without pretending to be an exhaustive list, the above table of troop movements between Folkestone and Boulogne in July 1915 gives some idea of the logistical issues involved in sheltering, feeding and transporting these men.

As they arrived at the harbour, the men, with full kits and rifles, formed long snaking queues to await their turn to board ship. There might be time to visit the buffet situated towards the end of the harbour, just beyond the station platform. Staffed by volunteers, the most dedicated of whom were the sisters Florence and Margaret Jeffrey, the departing soldier could expect a friendly, and free, cup of tea and cake. Also provided on a table in this cramped but hospitable room was a visitors' book. This remarkable book has

Folkestone Harbour. Photographed from an RNAS airship, the snaking lines of troops destined for the Western Front can be clearly seen.

recently been discovered in the East Kent Archives and contains many thousands of names, with the signatures of famous generals alongside those of the humblest privates.

The crossing to France was aboard one or more of the commandeered pre-war cross-channel steamers owned by the South-Eastern & Chatham Railway. Four ships, crewed by their pre-war merchant sailors, undertook the brunt of this work: *Onward* and her sister ship, *Queen*, together with *Invicta* and *Victoria*. As they cast off from Folkestone, the troopships would be met by their escorting destroyers and airships from the Dover Patrol. Upon arrival at Boulogne the men would be marched either to a local rest camp or directly to the station, for a train which would take them to the rear positions ready for the final march to the support trenches of the front line.

Rest Camps, Recreation and Religion

Although towards the end of 1915 the same chorus was heard, 'It will be over by Christmas', there was little confidence in the prediction. The Battle of Loos in September had not created the hoped-for breakthrough, and during the winter months plans for fresh offensives in 1916 were being worked out. Learning from the mistakes at Loos, the military planners were

HM Troopship Victoria *in her camouflage paint.*

confident that the next assault would be a success. Preceded by a massive artillery bombardment to crush German resistance, the infantry were expected to face little opposition as they marched across No Man's Land to secure the enemy trenches. As history tells us, the Battle of the Somme, which began on 1 July 1916, did not work out as planned. It was the first test for many of Kitchener's men and, though they lacked not in courage, many of them were sacrificed for little more than a few yards of muddy ground before the fighting ground to a halt in November.

In Folkestone the number of troopship crossings increased, with more young men being sent to fill the gaps at the front as the losses inexorably mounted. The war of attrition had set in.

To cater for the soldiers stopping off en route to the front, the idea of rest camps was conceived. Their main benefit would be to keep units together under one roof nearer to the harbour. They would also have beds, canteens and shops and would be a haven for the men before their departure. The first was erected in January 1916 in Marine Terrace, literally a stone's throw from the harbour, and slept 2,200 men. Rest Camp No. 2 went up five months later off Bathurst Road, with tents equipped with a stove and a large YMCA hut. The largest camp was No. 3, which opened in early 1917 and took in a large area of the Leas, including Clifton Crescent and Earls Avenue, and which catered for 5,000 men. At their peak, the camps were seeing in excess of 10,000 men passing through every day. Despite their lack of architectural charm, the rest camps were a blessing for the men, for many of whom it was to be their

The rest camp on the Leas in Folkestone, together with the canteen shop, selling everything from sweetheart brooches to foot powder for combating trench-foot.

last time on English soil. As they set off for war each man was given a copy of either the New Testament or the Book of Psalms. As one Folkestone resident noted, there was a distinct change from the early days, when the men marched cheerily along the Leas and down Slope Road to the harbour, singing songs and waving to the crowds along the route. Now, the crowds had gone and the men marched quietly, just the sound of their boots to mark their passage. In each man's mind must have been the question: will I come back home?

On the home front, it remained the government's intention to continue with 'business as usual', and Folkestone did its best to maintain this myth. Every edition of the *Folkestone, Hythe and Sandgate Herald* carried a column of local men killed, missing or wounded, together with stories of acts of bravery, and letters from men at the front, often describing their circumstances with reassuring, but probably false, bravado. On the other hand, the same local newspaper continued to advertise the new season's fashions, and all the trappings of normal daily life. Indeed, some advertisements seemed completely incongruous against the news of the carnage taking place just over the Channel. Within four days of 1 July 1916, the start of the Battle of the Somme, a full-page advertisement announced the grand opening of the Hippodrome, Circus and Zoo at Linden Crescent, Folkestone. Featuring Rossi's Troupe of Performing Elephants, clowns galore, horsemanship and a bucking mule, this must have been a panacea for those wanting to forget the war. But it seems that people did not want to forget the war; within a few weeks the Hippodrome went into liquidation. On the other hand the response was overwhelming when the Electric Theatre in Grace Hill managed to secure a copy of the film, *The Battle of the Somme*. The film was trailed as depicting the great victories and was being shown at cinemas across the country even as the battle was continuing.

Later in the season, the Pleasure Gardens Theatre was able to proudly present, direct from London's Apollo, a new musical comedy, *Toto*, starring Louis Bradfield, Enid Sass and Doris Lee. Just before the two-week run of

An advertising card for Toto, *the musical.*

Toto, on Sunday 8 October, the Pleasure Gardens hosted a performance by the Canadian (Mounted) Massed Bands, with a full programme of military and popular music. Although there was no objection to a military band performing on a Sunday, some of the other entertainments on offer led to clashes between the town's religious leaders and impresarios.

The contribution that the Canadians made to local life and, in particular to keeping up morale, cannot be underestimated. Barely a week went by without concerts being held in one of the town's four bandstands (three along the Leas and one on Marine Parade). During the summer months the Canadian Sports Day at Radnor Park attracted massive crowds, as did the boxing matches and baseball games. A particularly popular event was the Beauty Show held on the Victoria Pier. The catcalls and whistles from the mixed audience were explained when it was revealed that all of the contestants were Canadian soldiers, with Drum Major Morley carrying off the winner's prize of £2.

The Canadians had activities provided on camp, but they were also welcome to take part in local recreation and events, and took full advantage of the eclectic mix of offerings. Private George Broome of the 32nd Infantry Battalion (Manitoba and Saskatchewan) found time to learn a new skill. From Risborough Barracks he wrote to his mother in Canada: 'We have had nice weather here till today and it's raining cats and dogs. We are fixed up alright though. We are in huts. About 30 men live in each hut and have their beds and tables and chairs and crockery. The food is brought from the cookhouse and we eat right in our huts. They are pretty big although the name makes one think they are small. I believe I told you we are near Folkestone. We go there nearly every night. I am learning to roller skate. It is great fun although kind of rough for a learner.' Private Broome left for France in early 1916. He was wounded but returned to active service when, on 9 April 1917, he was wounded again at Vimy Ridge. He was shipped back

The canteen at the Eddie Wood Institute, Shorncliffe. The menu includes fried egg, corned beef, custard and jelly.

to a military hospital in England but six months later, at the age of twenty, George Broome died of his wounds. For Captain James Evans, also of the 32nd, relaxation was found not on the skating rink, but in music, as he described in a letter home to his wife: 'My own darling girl, Yesterday afternoon three of us officers went to the Leas and heard a Band concert by the Band of the 9th Reserve Cavalry – it was lovely. After that we had tea at the Grand Hotel and more music by the Orchestra and then to the Parish Church in the evening, beautiful singing by a boys' choir.'

In his letter to his wife, Captain Evans mentioned the Parish Church. As well as providing for the spiritual needs of townsfolk, visitors and soldiers, at the suggestion of the Chaplain of Shorncliffe Garrison, the Reverend R Deane Oliver, the churches of Folkestone set about providing places for the soldiers to congregate and relax. The first Soldiers' Club was opened at the Woodward Institute on the Bayle in August 1914, followed by another at Holy Trinity in October, and many more followed. The soldiers could expect a warm welcome from the Club helpers and they could buy postcards, cigarettes, confectionery and soap. Non-alcoholic drinks and snacks were served at competitive prices. On a busy evening at the Woodward Institute as many as fifty loaves of bread, one thousand teas and six hundred eggs would be consumed. Activities at the Clubs ranged from religious services to musical and concert party evenings, with billiards and table tennis for the more energetic.

Despite the efforts of the churches, concern was expressed by the military authorities that on Sunday evenings the men seemed unwilling to go

Mr and Mrs Mummery and helpers from the Radnor Park Congregational Church.
They provided not only religious worship, but also light entertainment, food and games
for the soldiers.

to the conventional church services and were roaming the streets. In
response, the Radnor Park Congregational Church decided to offer a less
formal service, with a good helping of secular music, including instrumental
and military bands. During 1916 the men flocked to the services and
remained for the rest of the evening to enjoy the facilities of the Soldiers'
Club, run by T A Mummery, his wife and helpers.

Postcard Home

Sept 24th 1916 Folkestone

Dear Miss Forrest,

Perhaps you would not mind favouring me again on Wed. Just come in from a walk along where this is a view of. It's lovely up there high above the sea. Lots of summer frocks about and sunshades for it's a glorious day. We hear one Zepp was brought down last night and another reported – that's good news. About six of our aeroplanes have gone over here this morning, full speed to France. It takes them 14 minutes.

    With love RA

The Cocaine Scandal

As we have said, the presence of the Canadians in Folkestone (they also had a strong presence in Dover, Hythe and Lydd), had a profound effect on the town. History tells us that such an 'invasion' by so many soldiers upon a civilian population is usually a recipe for disaster. We believe that the evidence shows that, in this case, the reverse was true – the relationship between the troops and the local population was mutually beneficial, and the general behaviour of the men was exemplary, such that General Sir Sam Hughes was able to remove the military police from patrolling Folkestone, and to place his soldiers on trust. Of course, with so many men passing through, there were occasions of discord, and a predictable crop of crimes, ranging from dishonesty (a great number of Canadian army boots seemed to find their way onto the feet of civilians), desertion, and an outbreak of bigamy.

    Perhaps the most notorious incidents involved Canadian soldiers supplying and using hard drugs, which ultimately led to the sale and possession of many of these being made illegal. Before the Great War many dangerous drugs were freely available, if you knew where to find them. Francis Chester had been both a drug user and dealer in New York before joining the Canadian Army and, when he arrived at Shorncliffe in October 1915, fighting was the last thing on his mind. During his frequent spells of going AWOL, he made for London to buy his supplies of cocaine to sell on to fellow soldiers at Shorncliffe. He found 'junk' being sold around Shaftesbury Avenue 'secreted in the packets of postcards of "Views of London" which were so popular with Dominion visitors. One packet cost only 5s. One woman pedlar told me she sold ten times more "snow" than she did morphine, and it was only the Colonials who used it, except some of the ladies of pleasure.'

    So great was the problem that in January 1916 a Canadian major at Folkestone reported that at least forty of his men had become drug addicts.

An operation was mounted to try to catch the dealers and a corporal succeeded in obtaining the necessary evidence, buying packets of 'snow' from Horace Kinsley and Rose Edwards, a London prostitute, for 2s. 6d. per packet. With hard evidence the pair were charged with 'selling powder to members of HM forces with intent to make them less capable of performing their duties.' Although the facts did not, frankly, come within the offence charged, that inconvenience seems to have been overlooked and the two dealers were convicted and sentenced to six months' hard labour. As a result of the Folkestone case and another high-profile case in which a drug-crazed Canadian officer, George Codere, bludgeoned to death a canteen sergeant, urgent steps had to be taken to curtail the sale and use of hard drugs. On 28 July 1916, regulation 40B, Defence of the Realm Act, came into effect prohibiting the possession of cocaine and other drugs without a prescription.

Mutual Respect

The most tangible evidence of the high regard felt by the people of Folkestone and Hythe for their Canadian guests can be found in a ceremony which first took place in 1917. By then a number of Canadian soldiers had died and been buried in Shorncliffe Military Cemetery, and a proposal was published in the *Hythe Reporter* by its editor, Edward Palmer, for a Canadian Flower Day. The idea took root immediately and, with children drawn from schools across the district, a service was held to honour these men. Not all of the Canadian soldiers buried at Shorncliffe died as a result of wounds received at the front. Some died in the Great Air Raid of May 1917, others from accidents and illness, and a few may have been suicides. William Meehan was thirty-six years old when he volunteered in 1915. He had served in his local militia in New Brunswick for the past ten years and he answered his country's call to arms despite the pleas of his wife, Alice, and their three young children. Private Meehan was assigned to the 23rd Infantry Battalion and sailed for England with the rest of the Canadian Second Contingent in spring 1915. Sadly, William succumbed to meningitis soon after his arrival at the barracks on Dibgate Plain and, although transferred from Shorncliffe Military Hospital to Folkestone Isolation Hospital on 14 August, he died from the disease three days later and was buried at the Military Cemetery (Plot N.288). Fittingly, the rolling hills of the cemetery, with the sea as a backdrop, bear a striking similarity to William's birthplace in St John, New Brunswick.

With an interruption during 1939–1945, the ceremony at Shorncliffe has continued to this day. Held every year on Canada Day, this poignant event is

William Meehan and his wife on their wedding day. William is buried in Shorncliffe Military Cemetery.

still attended by local schoolchildren, one child for each of the 296 Canadian graves. After hymns and prayers each child, many of whose parents and grandparents have carried out the same simple act, lays a posy of flowers upon the headstone of his or her soldier.

As far as we can tell from their letters home, most of the Canadian soldiers seem to have been left with a positive impression of their stay in and around Folkestone. The only thing they do not seem to have enjoyed was the weather. Another indication that they must have been made welcome is that, when the Canadian army finally left the town at the end of the war, they presented eight stained-glass windows, to be installed at Shorncliffe Station. The following poem, by Private Charles Davies from Winnipeg, appeared in a Canadian newspaper in 1919 and perhaps summed up the feelings of many of the men for whom Folkestone had been 'home' during the years of the Great War.

Shorncliffe Camp

Folkestone, thou Queen of the Southern Coast,
I'm loath to leave your grassy warren;
Those steep white cliffs that beacon like a genial host
Receding from my eyes nigh dim with tears.

What soothing hours and happy days so dear does memory recall;

Canadian Flower Day around 1920. It is still held on Canada Day every year to remember the Canadian soldiers buried at Shorncliffe.

The walk along the Leas, the leafy undercliff, and Oh, that changing sea,
When the rich red sunset sparkles on thy face,
Such are my thoughts of thee picture of grace.

Garden of England! Brave Men of Kent!
Think of your heritage: the flowers' sweet scent,
That wooded glade at Seabrook, primrose clad;
The glimpse of moving picture shore to make you glad.

Those verdant meads of Shorncliffe Plain,
Bright green as emeralds after rain.
Deep down in mist of blue lies sleeping Sandgate town,
Whose twinkling lights shine like some fairy's crown.

St Martin's spire, 'neath which brave Plimsoll sleeps,
Whose noble work the British sailor reaps;
The bugle blasts and all war's grim array,
Much as it did in Moore's far distant day.

Not even the mists of Passchendaele and its blood strewn duckboard track
Can blot from out my memory the charm of Radnor Park.
Who would not fight for thee, dear land,

For every flower and Kentish maid's fair hand?

Who cares for the muddy trenches and the shrapnel's piercing
scream,
The waves of poison and all the ghastly scene?
There are those away in the Golden West dearer than Nelson's name
Mothers and wives and sisters; it's for them we play the game.

The *Sussex* Incident

Folkestone bore its fair share of tragedies during the war but, apart from the
Great Air Raid in 1917 (see Chapter 4), these were of little interest to the
country at large, and even less to the wider world. For example, the loss of
the *Queen* on 26 October 1916 caused great sorrow locally because of her
long association with Folkestone as a pre-war cross-channel steamer, but the
sinking of one more ship, especially where no lives had been lost, was not a
matter of great general concern. On the other hand, the torpedoing of the
Sussex caused international outrage, and was ultimately a key reason for the
entry of the United States into the war.

Although the port of Folkestone had become a principal embarkation
point for troops, there was still a very limited civilian service running. At
1.25 pm on 24 March 1916 the steamer *Sussex*, with 388 passengers and
crew, cast off from Folkestone bound for Dieppe. The passengers were all
civilians and included fifty Americans and the celebrated Spanish composer
Enrique Granados and his wife. Once clear of the harbour the *Sussex* passed
through the Folkestone Gate then turned south on a route well away from
that taken by warships. At 2.50 pm the ship was ten miles from Dungeness
and, with a smooth sea and clear weather, a number of passengers were on
deck to enjoy what should have been a pleasant trip across the Channel.
Captain Mouffet was on the bridge with the first officer and the boatswain
when they suddenly saw a shimmer in the water about 150 yards off the port
side. It was clearly the wake of a torpedo and, unbelievably, it was heading
straight for the *Sussex*. Despite immediate attempts to alter course, the
missile struck the hull just forward of the bridge and exploded, destroying
the forward part of the ship, as far back as the first watertight compartment.
With no other vessels in the area, and the ship's wireless equipment
damaged, it was some time before rescue ships arrived. Miraculously, the aft
part of *Sussex* remained afloat, but many were killed in the initial explosion
and others drowned when thrown into the water. Among the dead were
Enrique Granados and his wife, who had been in their cabin in the forepart
of the ship. Help did arrive and the remains of the *Sussex* with her survivors

were towed into Boulogne.

An investigation was immediately launched and, when fragments of a German-made torpedo were found embedded in the debris, the finger pointed firmly towards the U-boats. With an announcement by Germany that UB-29, out of Zeebrugge, had sunk a minelayer at that location and time, there remained no doubt.

The furore following the attack on the *Sussex* led to an ultimatum being issued by the American President, Woodrow Wilson, in the following terms:

> I have deemed it my duty, therefore, to say to the Imperial German Government, that if it is still its purpose to prosecute relentless and indiscriminate warfare against vessels of commerce by the use of submarines, notwithstanding the now demonstrated impossibility of conducting that warfare in accordance with what the Government of the United States must consider the sacred and indisputable rules of international law and the universally recognized dictates of humanity, the Government of the United States is at last forced to the conclusion that there is but one course it can pursue; and that unless the Imperial German Government should now immediately declare and effect an abandonment of its present methods of warfare against passenger and freight carrying vessels this Government can have no choice but to sever diplomatic relations with the Government of the German Empire altogether.

Germany responded with what became known as the 'Sussex Pledge', by which they would stop the indiscriminate sinking of non-military ships. Instead, merchant ships would be searched and sunk only if they contained contraband, and then only after safe passage had been provided for the crew and passengers. The Pledge held good only until February 1917, when Germany reverted to indiscriminate attacks on shipping, in the hope that Britain would be brought to its knees. Instead, the abandonment of the Pledge, linked with the British interception of the Zimmerman Telegram, in which Germany proposed an alliance with Mexico against the United States, became a key reason for the United States declaring war on Germany on 6 April 1917.

The Chinese Labour Corps

During the years of the Great War, Folkestone played host to countless nationalities. We have mentioned the Belgians and Canadians. Americans were based there from 1917, and many others from the four corners of the British Empire passed through. By far the most unusual visitors, and about whom very little has been written, were the Chinese.

The arithmetic of war was simple: if the Allies could continue to replace men killed and wounded more readily than the enemy, they would win. It was called attrition. The problem for both Britain and France was that finding men to replace the casualties became more difficult as the war dragged on. If the men needed to carry out the jobs behind the lines, necessary jobs like repairing vehicles, maintaining roads and railways, loading and unloading ships and trains, could be released from those jobs, they could be moved up the front to fight. The solution, adopted both by France and Britain, was to recruit men from abroad who would be employed as labourers. British recruitment in China began early in 1917 and before the end of the war approaching 100,000 Chinese were signed up for service with the Chinese Labour Corps.

Britain recruited men from many places, including Africa, Egypt and India. Recruitment in China concentrated on attracting farming classes from Shandong and Zhili provinces. The men, who would not be required to fight or to enter combat zones, were offered a bounty on signing up of 15 Chinese dollars. Once he had passed his medical examination the recruit was kept in camp to await transport to Britain. The ships brought the men to Plymouth, from where they were sent by train to Folkestone, before being sent to France. A large camp was built for the men beside Cherry Garden Lane, under the shadow of Sugarloaf Hill. Records show that over 94,000 Chinese passed through Folkestone in this way, but there remained a steady number of some 2,000 Chinese in the town, and they were employed at the various military hospitals in the area and in general manual work at Shorncliffe Camp.

The men were carefully chaperoned, and kept strictly to camp when not working, and there is little evidence of the people of Folkestone being aware of their existence. When the war ended, the vast majority of the men were given passage back to China. The only evidence that they were ever there is to be found in a corner of Shorncliffe Military Cemetery where five headstones stand (one having fallen and been removed), marking the graves of a handful of men.

From the sparse evidence it is clear that the Chinese maintained their own colourful traditions, festivals and ceremonies, as revealed in the following letter:

> To my wife, Zhilan, I had intended to write to you earlier; however, it is only now that I have found a gap in my daily routine to do so. We are still at the same base camp. On the 13th it was Duanyang Festival [the Dragon Boat Festival] and we had the day off. The [Chinese] workers

The Chinese Labour Corps. Many Chinese passed through and worked in Folkestone during the war. Six are buried at Shorncliffe Military Cemetery.

were made up and put on the Yangke dance [a northern Chinese country peasants' dance] along the street. It was a very good show, but the foreigners seemed somewhat bemused by the event.

Some British Army [officers] came along and they brought with them some other [Chinese labourers], from the Hong clan from the west of Tai [the area around Tai Shan]. I will stop writing now, my spirit will follow the letter to you. My greetings and best wishes. Your clumsy husband Zhong Yangchong.

1918: Another Year of War

As we will see in Chapter 6, after four years of war, cracks were beginning to appear in the fabric of British domestic morale. No one was saying, as 1917 drew to a close, 'It will be over by Christmas', and not even the optimists thought it would end before 1919. Maintaining public support for the war effort, 'the battle for hearts and minds', became a critical part of government strategy, and this was achieved by a combination of stick and carrot. The stick came in the form of prosecutions under Section 1 of the Defence of the Realm Act, which prohibited 'the spread of false reports or reports likely to cause disaffection to His Majesty', while the carrot was much more subtle, including posters and postcards with patriotic themes and a firm grip on the way news of the war was reported in the newspapers.

In the autumn of 1917 a photographic exhibition was held in Folkestone's Museum and Art Room at Grace Hill. This was no ordinary exhibition, but displayed graphic pictures of the war, which had recently been exhibited at the Victoria and Albert Museum. Ostensibly to raise funds for the war effort, the images of death and destruction would have convinced any waverers of the need to fight on.

One of the most important efforts to bolster public opinion during this critical time was a visit to Folkestone on 15 February 1918 by Rudyard Kipling. The well-known author of *The Jungle Book* was a staunch supporter of the war, despite the loss of his son John, at the Battle of Loos in 1915. Kipling was not only a great writer but also a strong orator and his speech was filled with passion and warnings of what would happen if the war should be lost.

Postcard Home

46215. FOLKESTONE: THE WARREN.

19th July 1918 Shorncliffe
Daddy is at the seaside like Silloth and all the boats are waiting ready to take us over to France. Hope you enjoyed going to the Theatre last night.
Best love and kisses.
Daddy

The Sabotage of HMTS *Onward*

Before the Great War, the South-Eastern & Chatham Railway's cross-channel steamer, SS *Onward*, sister ship to the *Queen*, had sailed between the English and French Channel ports. Built to carry 400 foot passengers, she was the very first vessel to ferry a motor car from Folkestone to Boulogne, which involved the car being winched rather than driven aboard. In 1908 she collided with the *Queen* just off Folkestone, leaving her bow lookout mortally injured. With the outbreak of the war, *Onward* joined the ranks of His Majesty's troopships, often carrying over 1,000 men from Folkestone Harbour on their way to the Western Front. In November 1914 *Onward* had the distinction of bringing back to Folkestone the coffin of Lord Roberts of Kandahar; the 82-year-old general had been in France visiting Indian and British troops on the frontline when he died.

For the next four years *Onward* quietly and efficiently carried out her duties until, on 24 September 1918, she was the central character in a mysterious drama at Folkestone Harbour. As she was moored at her berth that morning awaiting the arrival of troops, a fire suddenly broke out which quickly spread to the saloon and threatened to engulf not only *Onward*, but also the stores and equipment on the harbour. The order was given to open her seacocks, and *Onward* rapidly settled and turned onto her starboard side, the flames being quenched with a terrific hiss. An investigation was begun as to the cause of the fire, but a detailed inspection had to await the recovery

The raising of HM Troopship Onward *in Folkestone Harbour in 1918.*

of the ship. It took divers a month to clear the masts and funnels, and in the meantime an ingenious system of tripods had been erected on the harbour. Cables were then attached to *Onward*, and were passed over the tripods and fixed to five steam locomotives acting in tandem to pull the vessel upright. The operation drew a crowd of spectators, among them the Reverend Carlile: 'Then the signal was given, and a miracle of science happened. The locomotives slowly steamed on till the cables were strained. The engines snorted and pulled in the fight with the dead weight of water until the old ship was slowly hauled into position and the water pumped out and the *Onward* again rode the waves.'

Investigators found evidence of the remains of a thermite bomb apparently hidden among the ship's lifebelts and, at the Court of Inquiry, it was concluded that *Onward* had been sabotaged, but by whom remains a mystery to this day.

In the Air

The skies over the south Kent coast must have provided a constant spectacle for those on the ground. As well as the Royal Naval Air Service aircraft and airships, the Royal Flying Corps (RFC) had airfields at Lydd, New Romney, Hythe (Palmarsh and Lympne), Folkestone (Hawkinge) and Dover (Swingfield and Swingate). The School of Musketry at Hythe also took on the role of training air gunners, with live firing exercises taking place on the Lydd ranges and along Prince's Parade, Hythe, where targets were towed

Hythe 1918. The Services Sports Day on the Corporation Fields. These young ladies are in the RFC and many wear the Penguin patch.

along the tramway. RFC personnel, men and women, the mechanics, clerks, drivers and caterers were all accommodated locally in billets, tents or barracks. Pilots and crews were accommodated in local hotels and homes. Hythe's Hotel Imperial was adopted as the main billet and mess for officers.

Walter Tull: Folkestone's Black Hero

Engraved on Folkestone's War memorial is the name of a remarkable man. Lieutenant Walter Tull was killed in action on 25 March 1918 while leading his men in an assault on German trenches at Favreuil on the Somme. Under heavy machine-gun fire, his men tried desperately to recover his body but were unable to do so, and his remains were never found. Walter's commanding officer later wrote, 'He was popular throughout the battalion. He was brave and conscientious. The battalion and company had lost a faithful officer, and personally I have lost a friend.' What makes his story remarkable is that Walter Tull was black. He was the first British-born black army officer and the first black officer to lead white British troops into battle.

Walter's father, Daniel, came to Britain from Barbados in 1876 and found work as a carpenter in Folkestone. He met a local girl, Alice, who was three years his senior, and in March 1880, when Daniel was twenty-four, they married. The couple lived in the town and went on to have five children, three boys and two girls, Walter being born in 1888. The family lived at 41 Walton Road and attended the local Methodist church but, in 1895, tragedy struck when Alice died following the birth of their daughter Elsie. With five children on his hands, Daniel then

Walter Tull (left), son of Folkestone, professional footballer and British officer.

married Alice's niece, Clara but, in 1897, he also died. Walter and his brother Edward were sent to an orphanage in London.

At the orphanage, Walter played football and it was here that he was spotted by a talent scout. In 1909 he signed as a professional for Tottenham Hotspur. In October 1911 Tull moved to Northampton Town, where he played half-back and scored nine goals in 110 senior appearances.

When the First World War broke out, Tull became the first Northampton player to sign up to join the 17th (1st Football) Battalion of the Middlesex Regiment, and in November 1915 his battalion arrived in France. Walter quickly rose to the rank of sergeant and, in July 1916, Tull took part in the Battle of the Somme. So impressed were his commanding officers that he was selected for officer training, despite military regulations forbidding 'any negro or person of colour' being an officer. Walter Tull received his commission in May 1917.

Lieutenant Walter Tull, the first ever black officer in the British army, was sent to the Italian front, where he led his men at the Battle of Piave and was mentioned in despatches for his 'gallantry and coolness' under fire.

Returning to France in 1918, Walter was again leading his men, in a counter-attack on the Somme, when he fell in No Man's Land. Attempts by his men to retrieve his body were unsuccessful, and he became one of the many victims with no known grave. Walter's name appears on the Commonwealth War Graves Commission memorial at Arras, and also appears on no fewer than three local war memorials, at Folkestone, Dover and River.

A Mother's Last Kiss

For Billy Poile the march down Slope Road was the last time he would set foot on English soil. William Francis Poile was nineteen when he received his call-up papers early in 1918, and, following basic training with the Royal Fusiliers, orders arrived to prepare to depart for the Western Front. After four years of conflict, the war in France and Belgium witnessed some of the

Private Billy Poile. He just had time for a final kiss from his mother.

most intense fighting, as the German spring offensive was halted and then pushed back. The pressure had to be maintained.

Billy's battalion, the 26th, was entrained for Folkestone, which was a bonus – that was his home town. Although his brother, Walt, was on active service in the RAF, and his father was serving on minesweepers in the North Sea, Billy hoped to get a spot of leave and be able to see the rest of his family. However, the young soldier's hopes were dashed. No sooner had the battalion arrived at Folkestone than orders were given to march to the waiting troopships. But all was not lost, as a kindly sergeant let Billy snatch a precious hour to visit his mother, Elizabeth, in their Denmark Street home. As he rejoined his comrades for the march along the Leas and down Slope Road, there, waving him off, were his mother and older sister, Eva.

On 6 October 1918, with the final prize in sight, Billy Poile was killed in action in Belgium. His CO wrote to Billy's family telling them that he had played a brave part in a long and victorious advance. 'He died instantaneously with no pain ... I was particularly sorry, because I had marked him previously as a keen smart boy with lots of grit.'

Billy's mother later wrote, '... it has made it much harder, because the dear boy didn't have any leave before he was sent over. But I am thankful that I was able to see him for that one hour and had his last kiss.'

William Poile is remembered on Folkestone's War Memorial and is buried at the Menin Road South War Cemetery.

Chapter 4

The Great Air Raid of 1917

The year 1917 will always be remembered in Folkestone for one event, the Great Air Raid. The war had touched the town in so many ways, and when there was heavy fighting on the Western Front, the guns in Flanders and France could clearly be heard. From the Leas could be seen the troopships with their Royal Navy escorts and, overhead, the airships of the Royal Naval Air Service (RNAS). Folkestone had opened its arms to the Belgian refugees and to the thousands of troops who had descended on the town. No one could say that the town was not 'doing its bit'. On the other hand, while so many other towns on the Kent and Essex coasts had been shelled or bombed, Folkestone seemed to have been left alone by the enemy. The mayor of neighbouring Hythe had voiced the belief of many when he wrote to a prominent London newspaper suggesting that this small area of Kent would continue to enjoy immunity from attack because of the aid given in 1878 to a stricken German navy ship, the *Grosser Kurfürst*, and the lavish memorial in the Cheriton Road cemetery erected by the town for the victims. For whatever reason, Folkestone had so far been left alone.

The Great Air Raid shattered Folkestone's sense of security,

Zeppelins cross the channel. A German postcard depicting a 'Zepp' raid.

and the shock wave was felt throughout the country. Such was the outpouring of anger that mobs took to the streets and attacked shops and businesses suspected of any German connection. The anger was also directed at the government and the military for seemingly doing nothing to prevent the raid. As we have already seen, the country had since 1915 suffered a number of air raids – so what was so different about the attack on 25 May 1917? The answer lies in the scale of the attack and the level of destruction wrought, particularly on helpless civilians. In this chapter we shall trace the origins of the Great Air Raid and, after following the enemy aircraft on their fateful journey, we will witness the horrors seen in the streets of Folkestone.

England had already been the victim of German air raids, mostly from Zeppelins, which had been dubbed 'Baby Killers'. Folkestone had only seen the enemy airships from a distance. There had been a raid on Otterpool Camp in October 1915. The town had a close shave on the night of 24 August 1916, when twelve German naval airships and four army Zeppelins set out for a raid carrying a total bomb load of 32 tons. While most of the raiders headed for London and its suburbs, L32 took an erratic course over the Kent countryside before heading for Folkestone. The spectacle was witnessed by many Folkestone residents, who had a grandstand view from the Leas. The Reverend Carlile was among the audience:

> It approached the town from the direction of Sandgate and floated on the breeze immediately down the Leas. When over the harbour it hung well up in the darkness as though poised for dropping its cargo of bombs. However, suddenly the searchlight from the top of Dover Hill shot its beam of light upon it, illuminating it from stem to stern. Immediately the guns crashed out, and the Zeppelin rose higher and higher, speedily making off towards the French coast, dropping its bombs with resounding crashes into the sea. The guns from Dover and from ships in the Channel took part in the fight, and a thrilling sight was presented to those who hurriedly went on to the Leas as the huge airship ran the gauntlet of the searchlights and bursting shells.

A month later, L32 returned on another raid. Perhaps owing to engine trouble, the airship suddenly appeared beneath the clouds as she headed along the Thames. As the enemy was picked out by searchlights she was pounced on by Lieutenant Frederick Sowrey in his BE2c biplane, who emptied two drums from his machine gun, causing L32 to burst into flames. The airship fell to ground near the Royal Flying Corps aerodrome at Snail's

British BE2c aircraft. Many were stationed at airfields across Kent to fight the menace of the Zeppelins.

Farm, Billericay, killing her entire crew. Interestingly, the ammunition used by Sowrey was called Brock-Pomeroy, designed specifically to ignite the hydrogen used in Zeppelins, and named after Frank Brock, whom we shall meet again in Chapter 7.

From the moment Germany had occupied Belgium in 1914, their High Command had seen the potential for striking at England from the air. It was part of the Schlieffen Plan that, when Calais was occupied, the invasion of Britain would be preceded by aerial bombardment. With London just 100 miles distant, even the early aircraft would be able to reach England's capital. The Germans came up with an imaginative cover name for the operation, 'Brieftauben Abteilung Ostende', which means 'Ostend Carrier Pigeon Detachment'. Although they were unable to set up base in Calais, aircraft of the BAO were established in Ghistelles in Belgium and it is likely that the early raids on Dover were carried out by the BAO. We do not know for certain, but it is possible that the German fighter ace Baron Manfred von Richthofen, the Red Baron, took part in these early flights; he was an observer with the BAO, before he went on to become a pilot.

Operation Turkencreuz (Turk's Cross) was the code name for Germany's plans in 1916 for the aerial assault on Britain. It was a simple matter of geography that, with the right aircraft, and operating from their forward airfields, London and other cities were within reach, while Britain could not retaliate. Our aircraft simply could not reach Germany. It was this strategic

Hauptmann Ernst Brandenburg. He was in command of the Belgian-based Kagohl 3, which flew many bomber missions against Britain.

advantage which had led to the Zeppelin attacks and, with the airships being neutralized, a new weapon was needed. The Gothaer Waggonfabrik Company promised that an operational aircraft would be ready for service late in 1916. The Gotha G.IV was a biplane powered by two 260hp Mercedes engines, carrying a crew of three and a payload of 300kg. Initially, thirty planes were delivered to the new bomber squadron, Kagohl 3, based in Belgium. Under the command of Hauptmann Ernst Brandenburg, hopes were high that the first attacks would be launched in February 1917. The principal target was to be London, but anywhere between Folkestone and Harwich could be chosen as secondary targets. There was a delay due to delivery and technical problems, but Brandenburg simply used the time to train his men and to perfect navigation and tactics, which would be all-important when up to thirty aircraft were flying in formation.

While Brandenburg was planning how to deal with English defences in the air and on the ground, we should look at what those defences amounted to. The first line of defence was the Home Defence Wing of the RFC, which was under Army control. Four squadrons were based around London and each had twenty-four aircraft, with responsibility to patrol a particular sector. Kent was the responsibility of 50 Squadron, with airfields at Harrietsham, Bekesbourne, Detling and Throwley. The aeroplanes available were the obsolescent types such as the BE2c, the BE12 and the FE2b, which had just about coped with the slow and low-flying Zeppelins, but would be hard pressed against the new Gotha. There were also the aircraft of the RNAS, which had airfields at Manston, Dover and Walmer, flying the more modern Sopwith Triplane and Pup, with Sopwith Baby seaplanes also based at Westgate, North Foreland and Dover. On the ground, there was a ring of permanent AA batteries around London, together with mobile units. Though the crews of the guns were well trained and determined, they were hampered by obsolete guns, ineffective range- and height-finding equipment and, most remarkable of all, an order which forbade inland AA guns from firing upon enemy aircraft. This order did not apply to the coastal AA guns, of which there were several along the south and east Kent coasts, though none of them covered Folkestone.

At the time of the Great Air Raid in 1917, Folkestone had no fixed AA guns. The few mobile units like this one were totally inadequate.

By the middle of May 1917, Brandenburg was at last happy with the performance of the Gotha G.IV aircraft and following a formal parade in front of Feldmarschall von Hindenburg, all that was needed was the right weather conditions for Kagohl 3 to launch its first attack on England. After some days of high winds and thunderstorms, the forecast for 25 May was positive, with cloudless skies over southern England and London.

With Brandenburg in his red Gotha, the armada took off and, just after 3.30 pm the twenty-two Gothas of Kagohl 3 crossed the Belgian coast, destination London. As they crossed the Essex coast the aircraft had reached their operational height of 16,000 feet. Their arrival did not go unnoticed and warnings were telephoned to air defence squadrons of the RFC, though there was little chance of their inadequate machines matching either the speed or height of the Gothas. The only British fighters which might be able to intercept the raiders were those of the RNAS, but they were not part of the Home Defence Wing. As they approached London, the German air crews may have wondered why they had not been assailed by AA fire; only one shot had been fired as they crossed the English coast. Had Brandenburg known of the order prohibiting fire on enemy aircraft, his next decision might have been different. The time was 5.30 pm.

At 4.30 pm the fast train to Folkestone from Charing Cross had steamed out of London with Mr E Turner in the cab. While the troop trains bound for Folkestone left from Victoria, there was still room on the South-Eastern

The Gotha G.IV bomber, like those which took part in the raid on Folkestone.

& Chatham Railway line for the odd civilian train and the 4.30 was filled with families planning to spend the Bank Holiday weekend by the sea. The town's Edwardian splendour might have lost its shine but it was 'safe', which was more than could be said for other pre-war favourites, such as Margate and Ramsgate, both of which had been bombed and shelled.

It had been a normal Friday, but the warmth of the early evening, and the promise of a sunny Whitsun weekend meant that many people were out and about. At Shorncliffe Camp men, mostly Canadians, had returned to their huts and tents after a day's training. The horse-drawn Hackney carriages and the Town Bus were drawn up at Folkestone railway station, ready to meet the arrivals from Charing Cross. In Tontine Street the road was thronged with shoppers, and a queue of chatting mothers and scampering children had started to form outside Stokes Bros, the greengrocers.

As Brandenburg led his Gothas over Tilbury he could see that London was covered with a dense layer of cloud. If he had known that, even had he flown below the clouds, he would not have met with a single shell from the AA batteries, he might have pressed home the attack, but instead he fired off his signal flares and the formation turned south into Kent. He had decided to strike for the secondary targets of Lympne, where the RFC had an aircraft park, Folkestone with its large army camp and the troopships in the harbour, and, to finish the sortie, the naval base at Dover.

The warnings which had preceded the German bombers when they first appeared over the Essex coast now broke down. In the belief that London was still the target, that was where the pilots of the RFC fighters sought their quarry. When the Gothas had veered south they had been hidden by clouds, and when they reappeared over Wrotham, heading towards the Kent coast, the vital warnings to the coastal towns had been overlooked. After dropping a few bombs en route, Kagohl 3 headed for the RFC park at Lympne where four bombs were dropped, causing some minor damage to the perimeter of the aerodrome. Although he was only supposed to be a ferry pilot, Lieutenant Gerald Gathergood jumped into an armed DH5 and took to the air to chase the Gothas. His aircraft was one of the best available but he would have to push the machine to its limits if he hoped to catch the bombers.

It took the bombers of Kagohl 3 only a matter of seconds to fly from Shorncliffe Camp to the town of Folkestone, and it was here that they dropped the majority of their bombs. At the controls of his train, Driver Turner had noticed the formation of aircraft passing overhead as he approached Folkestone. Being uneasy, he slowed down and halted outside the town and, as he saw the explosions ahead, he must have felt relief that he had made the right decision. Several missiles fell on or near the Central Station but several were duds and failed to explode. However, in Station Approach the unaccustomed noise was enough to frighten the horses of the Folkestone Station Bus, and it was only after a frantic dash that Driver Pilcher was able to bring them under control. Not so lucky

was Edward Horn, a butler in the service of Sir Thomas Devitt of Radnor Cliff. When the horses of a hackney cab parked outside the station bolted, he tried to stop them and he and the horses were killed as a bomb fell near to them.

But the finale of this day of terror was yet to come. A single bomb, probably a 50kg high-explosive device, fell in Tontine Street. The folk outside Stokes' greengrocer's had heard the sounds of the explosions and some would have seen the air-

Damaged houses in St John Street, Folkestone.

craft flying overhead. Even if they had not mistaken the noise for gunnery practice at Shorncliffe Camp, and even if they had not thought the aircraft were RFC machines, the throng of carefree women and children would not have had time to seek refuge. This bomb was not a dud. It exploded just outside Stokes', tearing down the shop and damaging many others. It killed sixty-one people outright and maimed many others. A gas main was damaged and burst into flames. In that moment Folkestone entered the history books.

The emergency services were quick to respond, led by Folkestone Borough Fire Brigade under the command of O H Jones. We can only imagine the scene that confronted them in Tontine Street. Folkestone's Chief Constable, Harry Reeve, said he would remember the scene until his dying day. Many of the reminiscences of that dreadful day focus, understandably, on the horror and carnage. Even the soldiers who joined in the rescue and recovery work could not be unaffected. Although he had

Stokes Brothers in Tontine Street. The scene of the greatest loss of life in the raid of May 1917.

Folkestone Borough Fire Brigade. In the passenger seat of the vehicle sits O H Jones.

been injured himself in the attack on Shorncliffe Camp, Konnie Johannsen
from Winnipeg went to help. He had joined the 223rd Overseas (XI
Reserve) Battalion in 1916 and had arrived at Shorncliffe just two weeks
before the raid. Konnie kept a diary of his wartime experiences and
described that dreadful day:

> Friday May 25th: Slept until 10. Got up and Tubs told us to get ready
> to move from Lower Dibgate to 11th. Arrived 11th at noon. Ate under
> shade of trees by road through 11th and 8th. Moved into quarantine
> tent and had just fixed up tent and finished our supper when 'Fritzers'
> raided us. One bomb dropped 15ft from us. Bill E, Bill, Tom, Hank,
> Davey and I all cut by flying glass. Raid lasted about an hour. Bill E and
> I hit for prairies and big oak tree. Helped girls over fence on way. Town
> of Folkestone, 2 streets blown to pieces. Holes out through our tent
> from Shrapnel. Left for Hospital 8.30 for anti-poison injection. Assisted
> carrying the wounded at Hospital. Had lunch at 11.30 (pm) there and
> then walked back to our tent. Could not go to sleep for a long time.

A factor that added to
the distress was that,
because many mothers
with their children had
been in Tontine Street,
almost entire families had
been wiped out. Surviving
relatives went to the
town's mortuaries with a
mixture of fear and hope,
where the task of ident-
ification was made more
harrowing by the con-
dition of the remains. A
local resident, Mrs Coxon,

*Shorncliffe Camp was also bombed during the raid,
killing eighteen Canadian soldiers. Here we see some
of the damage at the camp.*

wife of Commander Stanley Coxon, recalled: 'I was not there myself, but I
was told afterwards by a medical man, that it resembled a battlefield – a
gruesome sight of severed heads, arms, legs etc. mixed up with the wreckage
of broken houses and windows.' Even the Reverend Carlile, writing so soon
after the event, gave a graphic description of the scene: 'A ghastly, horrible
business of death and mutilation truly! The sights which met the gaze of
those who hastened to the grim task of removing the bodies and remains and
succouring the wounded baffled description. Human trunks were cleft in

Florence Rumsey. Know by everyone as Florrie, the 18-year-old wages clerk was killed instantly while working at Stokes'.

two or more pieces, heads were blown from bodies, and there were fragments of bodies and limbs whose identification was more a matter of surmise than anything else.'

A resident of Grove Road recalled: 'Some time later my brother, who was on leave from the Navy, came in covered in blood. He went to the sink and began scrubbing his arms. He told us he and his mates had been in the Clarendon in Tontine Street enjoying a pint when they heard the planes, and then a tremendous explosion. All the people around Stokes, the greengrocer's, were lying around, some of them screaming. There was nothing left of a pony and trap, or the farmer, from Hawkinge. There were no ambulances, but tradesmen brought their carts along and my brother and his mates set about loading them with bodies. The horses carted them all, alive and dead, off to the Victoria hospital.'

As the last of Kagohl 3 passed over Folkestone, Brandenburg steered a course for Dover, and it was here, for the first time during the entire raid, that any effective resistance was offered. The AA guns from Capel, Hougham and Langdon Battery as well as a number of the warships in the harbour sent up a barrage which was enough to deter the Gothas from pressing home their attack on the town. They headed out to sea and began the flight home. By now Lieutenant Gathergood, who had scrambled from Lympne air park, had caught up with the rear Gothas. Below him he had seen the trail of devastation and he was determined to even the score. He opened fire at close range, but had to pull away in frustration when his

Vickers machine gun immediately jammed. Another local pilot, Flight Lieutenant R F S Leslie of the RNAS took off from Dover in his Sopwith Pup and pursued the invaders over the sea. He also caught up with them and opened fire, pouring an entire tray of 150 rounds into one Gotha. Leslie then came under attack from several other Gothas and had to break off, but he had the satisfaction of seeing his victim billowing black smoke and descending towards the Channel.

For Germany the raid counted as a success. A brief communiqué was issued in Berlin the day after the attack: 'During the course of a successful raid one of our squadrons dropped bombs on Dover and Folkestone, on the south coast of England. Long distance flights inland also gave good results.'

In Britain the official report from Field Marshal French, Commander-in-Chief, Home Forces, while acknowledging that 'nearly all the damage occurred in one town, where some of the bombs fell into the streets, causing considerable casualties among the civilian population', went on to claim that 'Aeroplanes of the Royal Flying Corps went up in pursuit, and the raiding aircraft were engaged by fighting squadrons of the RNAS from Dunkirk on their return journey.' What was not explained was why the enemy aircraft had not been engaged either by defence aircraft or AA batteries during the 90 minutes that they had been flying over England. The failures in home defence exposed by this air raid led to demands for more and better aircraft to defend the home skies, and the embargo on AA batteries firing on enemy aircraft was lifted immediately.

For the people of Folkestone the task of counting the cost began – clearing the debris and repairing the damage, estimated at £20,000 and, of course, burying the dead. The anger also needed an outlet and this was found, partially, at the Coroner's Inquest. After hearing details of the first case, where Alfred Norris of Blackbull Road had lost his wife, Florence, along with his two-year-old daughter and ten-month-old son, the jury found the cause of the tragedy to have been: 'Death by bombs from hostile aircraft, Great Britain being in a state of war, and deceased at the time being a non-combatant.'

The collective grief of Folkestone was witnessed at a number of church services. On the afternoon of Sunday, 3 June, thousands of people thronged Radnor Park for an open-air service. The main memorial service had taken place the day before at the Parish Church, where the Archbishop of Canterbury, Dr Randall Davidson, gave the following address:

We are in, yes in, the great war. We are absolutely persuaded of the rightness, the inevitableness for men and women of honour, of what we did nearly three years ago, when duty and loyalty and truth compelled us to enter in it. Well, of course, we are not going to be simply flustered or frightened because in carrying our great cause through to victory, we are ourselves among those who personally suffer. We in this corner of England, on the Kentish coast, have the trust – would it be exaggeration to say the solemn privilege – of being the bit of England nearest to the enemy. We are proud of our sons and brothers who held the foremost trench in action on the Somme, or in defence of Ypres, or were first over the parapet. Someone – or rather some set of people – must be in the forefront. So far as English soil is concerned, the people to whom that special trust is given is we ourselves, we living here in Folkestone and Dover, and Deal and Ramsgate and Canterbury. We mean to be worthy of it and, please God we will.

As so often happens when such terrible events take place, there were

*Florrie's headstone
as it is today.*

instances of apparent miracles. These narrow escapes would have been desperately important to the townsfolk, whose faith in government to protect them had been challenged, as well as, perhaps, their sense of religious security in the midst of a 'just war'. It may be significant that each of the following examples, and a number of others, were recounted by the Reverend Carlile, a man who had much to do with maintaining the spiritual life of Folkestone during the Great War. When the roof and top floor of 28 St John Street were blown away, two women and a child who should have perished sustained only moderate injuries, as the structure above them hung in the air as if on hinges. Then there was the bomb which crashed through every floor of the Osborne Hotel in Bouverie Road West, before exploding in the basement, leaving every resident alive to tell the story. Finally, despite the devastation, much was made of the fact that, if so many of the bombs dropped had not been duds, the toll would have been far greater.

The final act of the Great Air Raid, as far as Folkestone was concerned, was the act of burial. The soldiers killed were buried with full military honours at Shorncliffe Military Cemetery. For many of the civilian victims there was a communal service and burial in a dedicated corner of the Cheriton Road Cemetery.

The Gotha air raids continued during the summer of 1917. The victims were south and east coast towns and, of course, the ultimate target, London. The daylight raids were followed by a series of night-time raids and many more lives were lost over the following months. Gradually, however, the English defences became more effective, so that the raiders were asked to make more and more sacrifices to press home their attacks. There were no more raids on Folkestone town but, with the newly installed air-raid sirens, there were plenty of alarms. There were close calls on 22 August, when Dover was bombed, on 25 September, when bombs fell just outside the town, and on 19 October 1917, when a wayward Zeppelin approached before being driven off with AA fire.

In Folkestone, memories of the Great Air Raid persisted for many years. Until the Second World War a memorial service, organized by the Salvation Army, was held each year at the site of the greatest devastation, Tontine Street. Even after the far greater carnage and destruction from air raids in the next war, the raid of 25 May 1917 still evokes a sense of horror and sadness. The reason is not hard to find. Until then the only risk for our island race had been assault from the sea, from which the Royal Navy had for centuries protected us. This new form of warfare, on unprotected and unprepared civilians, shook the nation to its core. The announcement by the

Home Office on 31 May 1917 that 'The tragedy at Folkestone will not be repeated anywhere if timely warnings can avert it' did little to restore a sense of security. The world had entered a new era of warfare and, for Britain, the wake–up call came with the air raid on Folkestone.

Chapter 5
Dover 1914–1915

Fortress Dover

Dover was not only an army garrison town, but also a Royal Navy base. The Admiralty Harbour was accustomed to the presence of warships, but during the few days before war was officially declared, activity in the harbour left little doubt that hostilities were likely to begin sooner rather than later. On 29 July 1914 HMS *Attentive* fired her guns and hoisted the Blue Peter, indicating that the warships in the harbour were preparing for immediate departure, and every sailor in town rushed to board his ship. New ships arrived: two scouts, four destroyers and seven C-class submarines. The next day HMS *Arrogant* arrived and she was to remain for the duration of the war, acting as a depot ship for the submarines. On 31 July a dozen Tribal-class destroyers arrived from Portsmouth to join the Sixth Destroyer Flotilla based at Dover. On the very day that war was declared, 4 August, a destroyer arrived in the harbour with two German merchant vessels captured at sea. The crews were detained at Dover Castle before being sent off to more permanent facilities.

On 8 August the men of the King's Own Lancashire Regiment, the Lancashire Fusiliers and the Inniskilling Fusiliers set sail for Calais as part of the 12th Infantry Brigade under the command of Brigadier H F M Wilson. Before the end of the month these troops were in battle at Le Cateau. As soon as the professional soldiers had left town, the men of the Kent Territorial Force arrived to start their training. By September the men of Kitchener's Army began to arrive, as did some of the refugees from Belgium, though most of these were diverted to Folkestone.

Dover became so busy with service personnel arriving and leaving that security became something of a nightmare. During the early days of the war, troop trains were arriving constantly with men destined for France and Flanders. This traffic was soon moved completely to Folkestone, while Dover took charge of receiving the hospital ships bringing the wounded from the front. This was clearly a sensitive move to avoid the demoralizing effect on outgoing soldiers caused by the sight of their wounded comrades.

To maintain security at Dover the whole town was designated a Restricted Area under DORA, the Defence of the Realm Act. In what might appear to be a curious move, the landward side of the town was ringed with newly dug trenches, with bombproof roofs; the curious aspect was that they faced not towards the sea, but inland. Their purpose was to enable the town to be held if the enemy managed to land an invasion force along the coast. The town and surrounds soon bristled with guns, as emplacements were built around the harbour and on the harbour walls to protect the anchorage, and anti-aircraft guns were placed at Cauldham, Citadel, Frith Farm, Langdon Bay, River Bottom Wood and West Hougham. The batteries were under the command of the local army commander, but within four weeks of the outbreak of war there sprang into being a volunteer force of local men determined to 'do their bit'. Many were members of the Royal Naval Volunteer Reserve (RNVR) or the Territorial Force, and they welded themselves into a useful adjunct to the regular forces. In particular, well over one hundred local men served as Searchlight Workers in their spare time. In

DORA arrives in Dover. To enter the town a permit was essential.

due course an unusual device appeared at Fan Bay, below Langdon cliffs. It was a sound mirror, a forerunner of radar, and enabled the sound of enemy aircraft to be detected before they became audible to the human ear. With the firepower available from the warships in the harbour, it is no surprise that the town became known as 'Fortress Dover'.

The speed of the arrivals and departures at Dover must have left the inhabitants in no doubt as to the strategic importance of their town. But even a town so used to soldiers and sailors could not be prepared for the next set of arrivals, the men and machines of the Royal Flying Corps. When the war began, the newly formed RFC, then part of the army, was deployed to reconnaissance duties in France and Belgium, while home defence, such as it was, rested principally with the Royal Naval Air Service. With the aircraft of this era needing little more than a relatively flat field to take off and land, a farmer's field at Swingate Lane, just behind Dover Castle, was chosen as the departure point for the first RFC machines to cross the Channel to join the BEF in France. Before departure, each pilot was issued with kit containing revolver, field glasses, spare goggles, water bottle, small stove, biscuits, cold meat and soap. A total of sixty-four aircraft from Nos. 2, 3, 4 and 5 Squadrons flew to Boulogne on 13 August 1914. They then turned south and followed the coast down to the Bay of the Somme, where they followed the old Napoleonic Canal inland to Amiens. This airfield at Swingate then became home to 62 (Training) Squadron.

The county of Kent was peppered with airfields before the war to cater for the boom in civilian flying. Most were commandeered by the government for military use within days of the outbreak of war. While the RFC was part of the army, the Royal Naval Air Service was the progeny of the Admiralty. This division of command was to prove an obstacle on many occasions to effective aerial home defence. The initial duties of the RNAS pilots were to provide support for the Dover Patrol and to defend the shipping in the Channel. There was already a large RNAS training school at Eastchurch on the Isle of Sheppey and additional facilities were established at St Mildred's Bay, Westgate, where both land- and seaplanes were based. At Dover the old skating rink at the harbour was converted to a seaplane slipway. Also at

Dover, the RNAS had an airfield at Guston, a stone's throw from that of the RFC at Swingate Lane.

Harold Rosher, RNAS, Aviator

Harold Rosher was posted to RNAS Guston at the end of 1914 and his letters to his parents tell us much about the lives and attitudes of the young men who have been described as 'the first of the few'. Rosher was born at Beckenham in Kent on 18 November 1893. As a child he suffered from asthma and this dogged him into his early adulthood.

Harold Rosher, Royal Naval Air Service pilot, stationed at Guston, Dover.

This may have been the reason why he opted for the open-air life by taking a course at the South Eastern Agricultural College in Wye, where he remained until the outbreak of war. On the day war was declared Rosher applied for a commission in the Royal Naval Air Service, and there followed various postings to training bases until, just after Christmas of 1914, he received his orders to fly to Dover to join his squadron. This journey was far from trouble-free, requiring a series of repairs, followed by more breakdowns, and getting lost in the clouds before arriving at his destination. The following letter from Rosher to his mother is full of incident and reveals the devil-may-care attitude with which this generation of young men became associated:

Hotel Burlington, Dover
30th December 1914

Dearest Mum,
Monday night some of us received orders to shift here the following morning. Two went off before me, as I burst a tyre to begin with – rather a bad start. In my second attempt I got well off, but found my air speed indicator was not working and my compass dud, so came down again. As I could procure no more, I decided to start. I nearly upset getting off, as my foot slipped on the rudder, and I got a bump at the same moment. The engine was going none too well, but I pushed off towards the coast, and all went well for a time. Then came signs of engine trouble. The revs dropped … and she missed badly and back fired. I at once shut off petrol and volplaned down from 4,000 feet. I glided two miles before I could find a field to satisfy me. Some farm hands and two special constables soon turned up and informed me I was miles from anywhere.

It was awfully bumpy and pretty nearly a gale blowing. I was just going to land when I saw two red flags ahead to mark bad ground, and then a lot more. My aileron and warp control was useless. I just managed to flatten out and straighten up a little as I hit the ground sideways. Both wheels buckled right up and brought me to a standstill, myself quite unharmed, and the machine with wonderfully little damage. I was awfully annoyed, as I was very keen on pitching well at the end of my journey.

Love to all. Ever your loving son,
Harold

If Harold Rosher had arrived at Dover a few days earlier he might have regaled his parents with details of an incident which places Dover firmly in

The Burlington Hotel, Dover, where Rosher and many other service personnel were billeted.

the history books of aerial warfare. On 21 December and again on Christmas Eve, a lone German aircraft flew across the Channel. The machine was a Taube, flown on both occasions by Leutnant von Prondzynski. During his first sortie, his bombs landed harmlessly in the harbour, but on his return visit the airman achieved the distinction of dropping the first bomb on British soil. He missed his target, Dover Castle, but shattered a few windows in the town. The only casualty was Mr James Banks, who sustained some bruises, as he was knocked out of a holly tree from which he was cutting sprigs for the Christmas decorations in St James's Church. At the time the incident was treated with some light-hearted contempt. Little did people then foresee the death and devastation which would fall from the skies over the coming years. It is a curious fact that the Germans had claimed an earlier success, for which there are no British records, first when Leutnant Caspar was said to have bombed Dover in October 1914, followed by another phantom raid in November. Hot on the heels of these two non-existent air raids came a German submarine raid on Dover Harbour on the night of 12 January 1915. These claims were clearly part of the propaganda campaign which both sides of the conflict developed during the Great War, and they show that Germany was acutely aware from the outset of the strategic importance of Dover.

Der Flieger-Leutnant Caspar warf als erster in diesem Kriege Bomben auf Dover hinab.

German propaganda. The October 1914 air raid depicted here never actually took place!

The Cuxhaven Raid, Christmas Day 1914

While the Germans were scoring a propaganda coup with their Christmas air raids on Dover, Britain was also announcing a daring air raid on Germany, and it involved three ships from the pre-war fleet of steamships

The attack by submarine depicted on this German postcard did take place, but the shells it fired missed any vital targets.

Angriff deutscher Unterseeboote auf Dover in der Nacht
am 12. Januar 1915.

HMS Engadine. *Converted into a seaplane carrier, this pre-war cross-channel steamer saw distinguished service.*

which had plied the Folkestone to Boulogne and Dover to Calais routes. From the ships of the South-Eastern & Chatham Railway commandeered by the Admiralty, we have seen that three were allocated as Troop Transports operating between Folkestone and Boulogne. Of the remaining ships, three, the *Engadine*, the *Empress* and the *Riviera*, were sent for alterations to fit them for a much more novel and warlike role – they were converted into seaplane carriers.

The German air raids on Dover in December were by aeroplanes, but on the continent the newest weapons of war, the Zeppelins, had already wrought destruction on a number of towns, and in Britain it was feared that these great airships would soon be coming across the Channel. What was needed was to hit the Zeppelin bases; the problem was how to do so. British aircraft during the early days of the war simply could not fly far enough to reach them. The solution was to launch an air attack from the sea.

After a quick conversion at Chatham, which involved constructing platforms and cranes, the three ships, each with three seaplanes aboard, and with an escort of destroyers and submarines from the Harwich Force, set off on Christmas Day for the North Sea. Due to engine trouble, HMS *Empress* fell behind and was attacked by German aircraft and a Zeppelin. Her crew were quickly issued with rifles and managed to put up enough of a barrage to keep the enemy at bay. Despite fog, low cloud and sub-zero temperatures, seven of the aircraft were successfully launched. Although sometimes referred to as the first ever aircraft-carrier attack, the planes did not launch from the ships, but were lowered into the sea onto their floats. The primary target was the Zeppelin sheds at Cuxhaven and, despite heavy anti-aircraft fire, the attack was pressed home. The damage done during the raid was by no means great, but it demonstrated the potential for such seaborne operations and it prompted the German Navy to remove much of its High Seas Fleet from Cuxhaven to safer havens.

After this operation, the three ships were sent off for separate duties. HMS *Riviera* was attached to the Dover Patrol, where she took part in a number of operations. HMS *Engadine* took part in the Battle of Jutland in 1916, where her seaplanes were to be used to locate the enemy fleet. In what was the only full-scale naval battle of the Great War, *Engadine* distinguished herself by sailing into the thick of the battle to rescue the crew of HMS *Warrior*, and to tow the stricken warship out of danger.

SS *Montrose*, the Reluctant Warrior

Before the year ended Dover witnessed another curious incident, this time at sea. The harbour had been taken over completely by the Royal Navy and it was clear that to protect the warships from attack from German submarines additional defences needed to be installed. These included high-power searchlights and guns, and the western entrance to the harbour was to be guarded by two blockships – hulks which would be sunk and from which torpedo nets could be strung across the harbour entrance.

The obsolete steamer, SS *Montrose*, was purchased by the Admiralty at the beginning of the war and was sent to Dover for use as a blockship. All of her upperworks were removed and she was filled with ballast. All was ready for her seacocks to be opened and for her to take up her duties at the harbour's entrance. Things did not work out quite as planned. On 28 December 1914 a severe south-westerly gale got up, accompanied by a heavy sea. Torn from her moorings, the *Montrose* set off on a voyage through the harbour, which was packed with moored warships. Despite having no one to steer her, the escapee navigated herself to the eastern entrance to the harbour, coming within inches of, but not striking, any of the other ships. She then made for the open sea where the chase was taken up by a number of tugs and other vessels. Several attempts to get alongside were made without success, owing to the trailing torpedo nets. Eventually, the *Ceylon* managed to get close enough to enable the two unfortunate seamen who had been on board *Montrose* to jump to safety.

Further attempts to salvage the *Montrose* all failed and she eventually sank off the Goodwins, where her mast remained visible until 1963. Apart from her remarkable escapade at Dover, the SS *Montrose* hid a dark secret. In 1910 she had been the ship which Dr Crippen, the man who infamously killed and dismembered his wife, had boarded with his mistress to flee the country. Perhaps, with such a history, it is not surprising that the *Montrose* baulked at such an ignominious end, and chose instead to find her own resting place on the Goodwins.

Harold Rosher, 1915

The air raids on Dover just before Christmas had caused little damage and only modest concern, but for Harold Rosher they had a most unwelcome consequence, as he explained to his father:

Dover 20th January 1915

Dear Dad,
We each have our own machines at last. Mine is the actual machine that Sippe had on his stunt to Friedrichshafen. Our chances of getting out to the front are remoter than ever, and each of these silly raids puts us further back still. If old Rumpler hadn't taken it into his head to drop a bomb over Dover on Xmas day, we should in all probability have been on the other side by now.

In March 1915, Rosher got his way – he was sent to France. For the next few months his letters home are full of incident, with details of raids,

crashes, those who survived and those who did not. These, and his own close shaves, are described with apparent nonchalance, which prob-ably belied his true feelings. Significantly perhaps, he

Harold Rosher's crashed Morane, from which he walked away without injury.

did not tell his parents about his crash at the end of April. His Morane was a total write-off and he had to be pulled from underneath the wreckage. Remarkably, his luck was still holding and he walked away uninjured. In May Rosher had to return to England to collect a new aircraft and, because of adverse weather conditions, he had time to spend a night at the Grand Hotel in Folkestone, before flying out from Dover and back to France on 18 May.

As well as the land-based aircraft at Guston and Swingate, a seaplane base was created at Dover Harbour. The former skating rink was converted into a slipway for these ungainly machines. Early models were unable to get into the air if there was more than a ripple on the surface, flitting about from one end of the harbour to the other, like a seagull with a broken wing. But, as has happened throughout history, technological advances were driven by the need to be better than the enemy, and the seaplane benefited from this progress, becoming an integral part of the anti-submarine force based at Dover.

The Air Raid on Dover, 9 August 1915

During 1915, warnings and scares of air raids at Dover were more numerous than actual raids. There had been a close call on 17 May when Zeppelin LZ38 dropped bombs near St Margaret's Bay. This was a period of intense Zeppelin activity, but most of these giant airships were heading for east Kent, London or England's east coast. Such a raid took place on the night of 9 August 1915, when five of the latest German naval airships set out to attack London Docks and then the City. For one of the Zeppelins, L12 under the command of Oberleutnant Werner Peterson, the night did not turn out as planned. As his ship made landfall over Thanet it was caught by a strong southerly wind. Thinking he had been blown well north of Harwich, Peterson turned south and, steering a zigzag course arrived over what he thought was Harwich at just past midnight. In fact, he had arrived at Dover.

The night's events had been followed by Chief Petty Officer E S Oak-Rhind, RNVR, who was on duty at the North Foreland Lookout Post (part of the AA Corps) at Thanet. His log entries for the night are interesting:

Time	Source	Details
2135	2nd Army	Keep sharp lookout for Zeppelins attacking tonight. London time will be about 2300. If Lowestoft sooner.
2250	AA	Aircraft engines bearing north.

2255	Foreness	Reculver reports Airship steering eastward at 2245. Birchington reports Zeppelin overhead steering SE at 2248. Westgate (RNAS station) reports aeroplane 1212 left in pursuit of Zeppelin. North Foreland reports Zeppelin overhead steering seaward at 2255.
2300	AA	Aircraft engines still audible bearing NE.
2301	AA	Drifter just fired two white rockets denoting aircraft overhead steering seaward at 2255.
2305	AA	North Goodwin Light Vessel reports sounds of aircraft in vicinity of North Foreland, heard guns, saw rockets.
0005	AA	Heavy gunfire from westward, probably 15 pounders.
0020	AA	Zeppelin can be seen fixed in Dover searchlights. Dover guns in action.
0030	AA	Zeppelin dropping bombs on Dover Harbour.
1520 (?)	AA	Aircraft engines due south of Ramsgate. Zeppelin homeward bound.

Another person who reported on the night's events, though in less formal language, was Harold Rosher. He was on a brief visit to Dover to collect a new BE2c aircraft when engine trouble forced him to land at Eastchurch Royal Naval Air Station on the Isle of Sheppey. He wrote home on 10 August:

Dear Dad,
I don't seem to be able to get away from this damn war. Last night 'old man Zepp' came over here – 'beaucoup de bombs' – 'pas de success'. Two machines went up to spikebozzle him but, of course, never even saw him. A sub went up from Westgate and came down in standing corn. Have just heard that he has since died. I knew him slightly. We have a terrific big bomb hole in the middle of the aerodrome and numerous smaller ones at the back. Expect to be back in Dunkirk on Sunday next.
    Love to all,
    Harold

When Oberleutnant Peterson arrived over Dover, he dropped a total of ninety-two bombs, a mixture of incendiaries and explosives. Only three fell on land, injuring three civilians and causing minor damage. Another fell in the harbour, near to the trawler *Equinox*, killing one soldier. The rest seem to have fallen harmlessly in the open sea. No doubt the ability of the Zeppelin to aim its bombs accurately was hampered by the intense gunfire from Langdon Battery. From the ground the appearance of smoke led to the belief that the airship had been hit. This was not smoke but water ballast being released, but the gunners had indeed found their mark and a number of cells of L12 had been ruptured.

Peterson and his crew managed to limp home but their troubles were far from over. Landing in the sea just short of Ostend, they were taken in tow, but were then pounced on by fighters from RNAS Dunkirk. In the haste to get L12 into port, the German tug managed to break her back before bringing her alongside at Ostend Harbour, where, for reasons never fully understood, she caught fire and was utterly destroyed. So ended L12's first and only raid.

Harold Rosher's Return to Dover

Harold Rosher's tour of duty in France came to an end in September 1915. During his time there he had taken part in a number of raids, including at Ostend, Zeebrugge and Antwerp. He had also seen many friends and comrades perish. His last letter home from the front is apparently nonchalant even in the face of such risks:

9th September 1915

Dear Dad,
Very little news except that we had monitors bombarding Ostend the day before yesterday. It was a fine sight from the air. A Frenchman was badly hit in the leg going out there, but went on, dropped his bombs and got back. He is not expected to live. Four new subs have turned up here and I am going home as soon as they can fly the fast machines. I ought to have gone home by rights about 2 weeks ago. Am flying over when I eventually do come home. The last two machines that went over both crashed at Folkestone – shall probably do the same.
Love to all,
Ever loving son,
Harold

In the event Rosher did arrive back in England safely and returned to Guston aerodrome in Dover. He was soon promoted to the post of First

Lieutenant, which meant he was second-in-command, but almost as soon as he had landed he was angling to return to active service. Once again Rosher celebrated the New Year in Dover and he marked the occasion by looping his new BE2c aircraft. He was well strapped in but the cushion on the passenger seat fell out and vanished!

The Sinking of the Hospital Ship *Anglia*, 17 November 1915

In response to the ever-increasing number of casualties from the Western Front, the initial complement of four hospital ships at Dover was supplemented with the arrival of a number of merchant passenger steamers, *Cambria*, *Anglia*, *Dieppe*, *Brighton* and *Newhaven*. The fleet was marked in accordance with the Geneva Convention with the unmistakable Red Cross flag. The *Anglia*, under her Irish skipper Captain Lionel Manning, and with most of her merchant crew from the Holyhead service, arrived after her refit in May 1915. She and her crew set about their new duties with enthusiasm and they must have been proud to have been given the delicate task, on 1 November 1915, of bringing the King back from France after he had sustained injuries when he fell from his horse while reviewing troops.

The morning of 17 November 1915 dawned clear and bright, and a smooth crossing for the 386 casualties was expected. Casting off from Boulogne Harbour at 11 am, a little later than planned, *Anglia* headed for Dover, taking the route reserved solely for the hospital ships, which was marked by special buoys. As they approached the buoy just east of the Folkestone Gate, Captain Manning remarked to his men that they had made a beautiful crossing and went to fetch his gloves from his room. Just as he arrived back on the bridge, the ship was rocked by a massive explosion. Manning's first thought was to call for help: 'I at once jumped up and, going to the wireless cabin, ordered the wireless operator to send the SOS signal. I found his face cut and the room wrecked, and he explained to me that the apparatus was useless. I ran at once to the telegraphs to stop the ship, but found that they were broken by the explosion, and then hurrying to the voice tube I gave verbal orders to the engine room, but that was also broken. The ship was now very much by the head, and the starboard propeller was turning clear of the water.' In these few sentences Captain Manning has described the ultimate nightmare for a stricken ship: no communication with the outside world, none with the engine room, and the ship sinking bow first with her propellers still turning, thus driving herself under the waves. On top of this there were nearly 400 souls on board who could not fend for themselves.

For those who had managed to get into the boats, the collier MS *Lusitania*

The sinking of the hospital ship Anglia. *William Couzens was aboard HMS* Hazard, *which joined the rescue operation.*

(not the cruise ship of the same name, which was sunk on 7 May 1915) was a welcome sight as she hove into view. She had seen the explosion and turned round, lowering her own boats to help pick up survivors. Captain Manning described what happened next: 'Our boats at this time approached *Lusitania* with a view to putting their crews on board. Being on the lower bridge at the time, I saw them proceed to *Lusitania*, but as the first man started to clamber on board the rescuing vessel there was another explosion, and the *Lusitania* sank stern first shortly afterwards.'

The explosions had been seen at Dover, and two ships were sent to investigate, HMS *Ure* and HMS *Hazard*. On arrival at the scene, Lieutenant Boxer in command of *Ure* was faced with an almost impossible task: the *Anglia* was bow down in the water with her engines still running, one propeller was under the water making the stricken vessel turn in circles at an alarming 8 knots, and the other propeller was just a few feet above the surface turning like a giant circular saw. On the *Anglia*'s decks were sick and injured men whose only hope of rescue lay with HMS *Ure*. In a feat of outstanding seamanship and bravery, Boxer rushed towards the hospital ship and, matching her movements, got close enough for his crew to be able to manhandle many to safety. He repeated the manoeuvre, but seeing that there remained others clinging to the fast-sinking *Anglia*, he made a final dash and, positioning *Ure* across her sunken bow, he managed to take off all those still on deck.

Petty Officer William Couzens had joined the Royal Navy as a boy in 1893, gradually working his way up through the ranks, before joining *Hazard* in October 1913. *Hazard* was an old gunboat and difficult to manoeuvre, but her boats picked up many survivors who had jumped into the sea, and PO Couzens has left us with photographs of that dreadful day.

With their human cargoes aboard, HMS *Ure* and *Hazard* returned to Dover, and the task was begun of counting the costs and discovering what had happened. Given the circumstances, it was perhaps miraculous that anyone had survived that cold November day, but the number lost was still considerable, and there was worldwide outrage. Of the crew of *Anglia*, twenty-five perished, consisting of the Purser, four deckhands, twelve engine room men and eight stewards. There had been a total of twenty-five medical staff on board, including three female nurses. Of these, ten orderlies and one nurse, Sister E A Walton, were lost. Of the 386 injured officers and men who had left Boulogne and the battlefields of France for what they expected was the safety of home, five officers and 128 men drowned.

Captain Lionel Manning was found floating, unconscious, in the sea and was rescued. A man of few words, Manning later praised the work of his crew and those of the rescue ships. He also told the story of one of the RAMC nurses, Sister M S Mitchell, who was found up to her waist in water in B Ward trying to bring out a cot case. Lieutenant Bennett who found her helped to bring the invalid up to safety, but he then had to use force to stop Sister Mitchell from returning to the ward, where she would certainly have perished.

The cause of the disaster was quickly established. The German mine-laying submarine UC-5 had set a chain of mines around the buoy, which, as already mentioned, had been placed for the sole use of returning hospital ships. It might have been thought a terrible mistake by the captain of UC-5, but a communiqué issued from Berlin the next day made it clear that it was not. It was claimed that the British were using vessels masquerading as hospital ships for carrying combatants and munitions, though no evidence to support this claim was ever produced, and it was strenuously denied by the Admiralty.

The Railway Disaster of 1915

The history of Dover's railway network is unusual. Originally two companies, the South-Eastern Railway and the London, Chatham & Dover

Railway, operated in competition but in 1899 they agreed to set up a conglomerate, the South-Eastern & Chatham Railway. The result was that, just before war broke out, the town had three stations, Priory, Town and Harbour, with a fourth, Marine, under construction. The building of the Marine Station began in 1909 and, at a cost of £400,000, it was to be the centrepiece of Dover's appeal to the modern cross-channel traveller. In August 1914, before a single passenger was able to set foot on its platform, the entire harbour was taken over by the Admiralty. Add to this that the town of Dover became a Restricted Area, that Dover Town station was closed on 14 October (never to re-open), and it is little wonder that, almost overnight, Dover lost any pretensions as a holiday destination.

The wartime rail service at Dover was principally concerned with transporting the material of war and serving the hospital ships arriving from France. Seven ambulance trains were always on duty with another couple of engines stationed at the harbour to provide heating for carriages awaiting movement.

There remained a limited civilian service, and by this means sailors and soldiers from Dover could travel to Folkestone for recreation, there being little to be had in Dover, thanks to what was effectively a regime of martial law. Even this facility came to a sudden end on 19 December 1915, when the line between the two towns was destroyed, though not by enemy action. At 6.10 pm that day, the train from Ashford had just left Folkestone Junction. Getting up speed as the train entered Martello and Abbotscliff Tunnels, the driver was unaware of the catastrophe ahead – the cliff through which the line had been carved had started to crumble. Some way ahead three men of the King's Own Lancashire Regiment were on guard duty when they heard an ominous rumble and, on investigating, saw the rail track start to buckle. With no time to lose the soldiers ran back down the line to warn the train driver, who was able to halt the engine just in time. The passengers were swiftly evacuated and guided safely back to Folkestone by lamplight. Shortly afterwards the whole cliff face fell into the sea, with the locomotive and four carriages plummeting 30 feet. The Folkestone Warren Landslip was recalled by one of the soldiers, without whose quick thinking the outcome might have been tragic:

We were sitting about inside, and at about half past six on Sunday we heard a queer rumbling noise. I went out to see what was happening, and in the moonlight I could see that the cliff was coming down on top of us. It was a regular avalanche. Trees, shrubs and great chunks of cliff were crashing down right over the railway and into the sea. We thought it was time we cleared out, and we didn't worry about

The Warren Landslip in 1915 severed the rail connection between Folkestone and Dover.

taking anything with us. We just left.

Some of us went along the line with red lamps to stop trains, and it was a good job we stopped the train from Folkestone. All the people got out, and it wasn't long before some of the coaches were at all sorts of angles. The whole shore seemed to be on the move.

Sergeant Jackson of the KOLR was awarded £5 and his two privates each received £2, as did Lance Corporal Evea of the Devon Cyclists, who was first to raise the alarm.

To replace the rail service between Dover and Folkestone, a new route was created from Dover Priory to Folkestone Junction via Minster, Canterbury West and Shorncliffe. In view of its departure time from Dover of 5 am and return at 7.25 am, this service was not likely to attract the recreational traveller. Bus services were also provided. It gives some measure of how popular the bus route was that, although the bus fare was 9d. compared to 6¹/₂d. for the train, every one of the coaches running at half-hour intervals throughout the day was full.

The closure of the rail link between Dover and Folkestone seriously hampered the flow of military traffic, including the hospital trains. For Stanley Coxon, however, there was an added blow: 'Over and above this, the collapse of this branch line, which they now tell me is a permanent

LAMBERT & WESTON, DOVE

The Romps were popular with the troops in Dover.

one, has caused not only the greatest inconvenience to the two towns, but has put an end to even the smallest relaxations we once had. For, after all, war or no war, one must try to do something in one's time off. Here in dirty old Dover there is absolutely nothing, not even a theatre nor decent music hall, while in Folkestone you have a really excellent theatre, a good golf course, good music and a clean town. But nowadays you cannot get there, the only mode of conveyance being motor buses, which are generally full and always irregular in their running.' However, Coxon's damning judgement on Dover's recreational facilities should not be taken too much to heart, as there were several establishments which did their best to provide entertainment. These included the Town Hall, the King's Hall, the Duke of York's School, the Missions to Seamen's Institute, the Carriage Builders' Institute and the Tipperary Tea Rooms in Bench Street. According to Mabel Rudkin, 'Soldiers continue to figure at the recurring Temperance Teas, some assisting at the concerts. A dapper, swaggering corporal, sporting a smart cane, had a fine tenor voice, and was much in demand as a singer. He fluttered many feminine hearts with his melodious entreaties to "Keep the Home Fires Burning", and the rendering of other popular lyrics.'

The South-Eastern & Chatham Railway was keen to repair the line and, in 1917, a plan for a temporary repair was put to the War Office, but it was rejected as too expensive for government funding. By mid-1918 the railway company decided, as the land had remained stable, to go ahead and carry out the repairs. Curiously, when this plan was put forward, it was announced that the Admiralty wished to utilize the Abbotscliff Tunnel for 'important national purposes'. As the war came to an end shortly afterwards, the tunnels were never used by the Navy, and to this day it is not known what those purposes were.

Chapter 6
Dover 1916–1918

The Key to the Kingdom

The early expectations of a quick and decisive war had evaporated by early 1915, with both sides becoming entrenched in a line which extended from the Belgian coast in the north, through France and down to the Swiss Alps. The plans by the Allies for a 'Big Push' in 1915 had come to nothing at the Battle of Loos in September. During the winter months of 1915–16, British strategists, who believed that they had learned from the mistakes of Loos, started to put together an even bolder plan. They were planning the Battle of the Somme. It had not yet become a war of attrition on the Western Front, but the need to send more men and machinery to France and Flanders was obvious. If this was obvious to the British, it was equally so to the German High Command.

Dover was the key to Britain's ability to continue the fight in Europe, and the town, the harbour and the Dover Straits became pivotal to the success of mainland operations. Keeping open the sea lanes for troop and supply ships was the single objective, and this task fell to the Dover Patrol. The enemy was not going to concede the Channel without a fight and, as we shall see, was able to deploy a range of obstacles which, at times, seriously threatened to destroy this slender artery.

The Air Raids Continue

In the last chapter we considered in detail the air raid on Dover in August 1915, but despite the frequent false alarms the town had come through the first two years of the war relatively unscathed. But Dover's fortunes were about to change.

The catalogue of attacks began on 23 January 1916. A German seaplane from Seeflugstation Zeebrugge arrived over the town at 1.30 am on this beautiful moonlit night. Commander Coxon was at work decoding a cipher telegram when the explosions shattered the stillness, and his first thought was that enemy submarines had entered the harbour and were engaging the ships. As he and his wireless operator rushed out onto the Admiralty Pier, silence returned, but there was then a sudden sheet of flame erupting from the town. The single raider had dropped nine bombs on the town. Damage was considerable, including houses along the seafront and the Red Lion Inn in St James's Street, which had its roof blown off, killing Harry Staden the barman and injuring three others. In what was a bad night for the licensed trade, the malthouse of the Phoenix Brewery was also destroyed. Situated in Dolphin Lane, off Castle Street, the Phoenix Brewery had been part of the Dover townscape since 1740 and during the nineteenth century it had been just one of eight breweries in the town. By 1859, when the business was bought by Alfred Leney, the brewery had established itself as the main employer, outside the shipping and marine industries. During the Great War the Leney family did much to help the town. They used their office windows as a noticeboard, posting telegrams and other items of war news, including the telegram announcing the Armistice. During 1916–17 the company's Empire Palace Theatre was opened up for the use of troops. They also opened up their cellars and vaults as public shelters during air raids, though with the understandable proviso that a police constable should also be on duty at such times – just in case anyone should feel tempted to seek additional courage in the company's stocks!

A German postcard depicting seaplanes of the type which carried out early attacks on Dover.

The Market, Dover

Market Square, Dover. This busy, peacetime picture became simply a memory once the German air raids on Dover began.

Harold Rosher, 1916

For the first few weeks of 1916, Rosher's time was taken up with duties at RNAS Guston, where he was now second-in-command, with the occasional trip across the Channel to deliver new aircraft. The following letter home starts with his usual boyish enthusiasm, but then turned to the ever-present risk taken by these early aviators:

Dover 9th February 1916

Dear Mum,
Am still going strong. Flew four different types of machines today, two of them new ones, one a Shorthorn Maurice, and the other a Bleriot. The Bleriot is the first monoplane I have flown other than the parasol.
You have heard me mention Graham. Well, he has just had an awful bad crash at Dunkirk. Penley has also crashed badly twice out there, and is now back on sick leave. Ford too is home on sick leave with his head cut open, as the result of a bad crash, and his passenger is not expected to live. If one goes on flying long enough, one is bound to get huffed [killed] in the end.
Best love,
Ever your loving son,
Harold

Two days later Rosher wrote to his father telling him about a report of a German raid over Ramsgate. Although he took off in pursuit, the only other aircraft he came across was an RNAS seaplane from Westgate. In fact it was that plane which had been mistakenly reported as a German. After he landed, Rosher went to Capel le Ferne to visit the 'Blimps'. The squadron CO was due to go on leave during the last two weeks in February and Harold would be left in charge. He had to welcome over sixty ratings to the aerodrome and make arrangements for them to be housed and fed. They had been recruited in Derby and were mostly butchers, grocers, cotton-spinners and weavers. None had previously seen an aircraft, let alone worked on one.

The winter of 1915–16 was bitterly cold with heavy snow across the whole of Europe. For the soldiers in the trenches on the Western Front it was a bleak and miserable time. Back in Dover, although there was little flying, Harold Rosher also had to contend with the weather, as he explained to his father:

Dover 24th February 1916

Dear Dad,

Drove over to Eastchurch yesterday on business [there was another RNAS aerodrome there], roads in places 18" deep in snow. Coming back I had a priceless skid and finished up in a ditch. No one hurt or even shaken. Returned here by train, and car came on today. It was really rather comic.

Did you hear how Usborne and Ireland were killed? If not, I will tell you later. T— was burnt to death.

Love to all,
Ever your loving son,
Harold

Harold Rosher did not have the opportunity to tell his father how his colleagues had died. On Sunday 27 February he too was killed. One of his duties was to train fresh pilots on the new and faster machines becoming available. That Sunday morning he took up a newly repaired aircraft before allowing a new pilot to fly it. As the aircraft flew over the airfield it suddenly lost its trim and nosedived into the ground. Harold Rosher was killed instantly. A few days later he was buried in the town's Charlton Road cemetery with full military honours. Ever since Harold Rosher had taken to the air, he had been living on borrowed time. He and his fellow pilots knew this all too well – if they were not shot down in combat, they were likely to become victims of the frail machines from which they often demanded the impossible. Rosher and the other young pilots were sustained by their comradeship and, as they gathered round the mess piano in the evening, they mocked their fate in drink and song:

> The young aviator lay dying
> And, as 'neath the wreckage he lay,
> To his comrades assembled around him
> These last parting words did he say:
> 'Take the piston out of my kidneys
> Take the con-rods out of my brain.
> From the small of my back take the crankshaft,
> And assemble the engine again.'

The Sinking of P&O *Maloja*

On 27 February 1916, the same day that Harold Rosher met his death, an incident happened at sea which confirmed in the minds of many that the enemy was prepared to stoop to terror tactics and target helpless civilians to achieve victory, or at least to force the allies to the negotiating table.

> On Sunday morning at 10.30 the inhabitants of Dover heard a loud explosion, like that of a heavy gun. Those who were in view of the sea, saw a large P&O liner just to the west of Dover and a column of water and debris blow into the air from her stern. The Dover Harbour tugs *Lady Brassey* and *Lady Crundall* at once steamed to the vessel's assistance followed by many trawlers, dredgers etc. The vessel, which was the largest boat of the P&O line, the *Maloja*, was at the time proceeding at full speed. The end of the vessel was watched with intense anxiety by the assembling crowds on shore and twenty-four minutes from the explosion the vessel sank ... [*Dover Express*, 3 March 1916]

Stanley Coxon described the aftermath:

> Never as long as I live will I forget the sight which met my eyes as I came into the Lord Warden Hotel dining room for lunch on the afternoon of the day of the sinking of the *Maloja*. From 10 a.m. until 3 p.m. I had been disembarking the survivors and the dead and wounded of that ill-fated ship.
>
> Finding a young woman seated in the hall of the hotel, sobbing her heart out, I ascertained that she was looking for her husband to whom she had been wedded but recently. From 2 p.m. to 9.30 p.m. she had sat in that chair looking, every time the hall door opened, for the husband who never came. He was drowned, and his body was at the time lying in the mortuary, and I knew it. She wouldn't eat and she wouldn't

The cruise ship SS Maloja *pictured in 1912.*

drink, and she couldn't sleep, until, fearing a collapse I had to call the aid of some other ladies in the hotel, to get her carried forcibly upstairs and put to bed.

Another witness to the destruction of the *Maloja* was John Lawton, a lance corporal in the East Kent Regiment (the Buffs). At the time his battalion was on home duties guarding Dover, but in February he was in the Military Hospital on the Western Heights with a septic leg. He wrote home to his parents in Staffordshire:

This morning all was bright & peaceful, the bells were ringing & now & then a siren from the harbour was heard. At 10 o'clock the Angel of death & destruction was hovering very near us. Suddenly a terrific explosion shook the ward to its foundations. All those who were up rushed outside & were just in time to see a magnificent P&O Liner rapidly disappearing beneath the waves & now the report which I am afraid is only too true is that the hotel facing the pier is full of boatloads of casualties. It must have struck a mine. At the same time a tank steamer was sunk in the vicinity. When one is so near such terrible happenings it makes one realize to the full the grim horror of war & the truth of the scriptural proverb and epigram 'in the midst of life we are

As rescue ships race to the scene off Dover, survivors of the Maloja *cling to the wreckage.*

in death'. One moment a splendid liner crowded with passengers with hopes & aspirations like ourselves, breathing-in the pure sea air & thrilled with the joy of life. Next they are swiftly hurled into eternity & the liner is a thing of the past. Surely war is a frightful thing.

Many of the victims of the *Maloja* were buried in St Mary's Cemetery in Dover and, unusually for civilian casualties, they were given a military funeral. The event was covered by the *Dover Express*: 'The funeral procession left the Market Hall at two o'clock. It was headed by a firing

The burial of the Maloja *victims at St Mary's Cemetery, Dover. Although the dead were civilians, the ceremony took place with full military honours.*

party of the Royal Fusiliers and the band of the same regiment ... Crowds lined the route of the procession, but the Cemetery was kept free of spectators ... Amongst those at the graveside was Captain Irving, the master of the ill-fated vessel. After the conclusion of the service, the firing party fired three volleys and the buglers sounded the Last Post.'

More Air Raids

The next air raid took place in daylight on Sunday 19 March 1916. A squadron of German seaplanes based at Zeebrugge flew across the Channel that lunchtime, half heading for Thanet, where there were several fatalities, and the remainder making for Dover. The first bomb landed in the Admiralty Harbour and then three more in Northfall Meadow adjacent to the Castle. A hut occupied by men of the 5th Battalion, Royal Fusiliers was destroyed, killing four of them and injuring eleven. More bombs were then unloaded on the town, where the only targets were civilians. Edith Stoker was blown from her bicycle in Folkestone Road and suffered fatal injuries. Nearby was seven-year-old Francis Hall, who was on his way to Sunday School when he heard the noise. He turned and ran for home when, within sight of his mother who had come out to find him, the bomb exploded, killing him instantly. As bombs continued to rain upon the town, a good deal of damage was done, and several people were injured.

With the increasing number of raids on Dover, and many more false alarms, steps were taken to protect the inhabitants of the town, but they were piecemeal at best. There was no government strategy and it was left to the civilian authorities to do the best they could. A number of schemes were introduced: for example, Dover Town Council issued orders for dugouts to be constructed for the civilian population. The first to be excavated was in Connaught Park. Initially intended as a shelter for children playing in the park during daytime raids, it later became a popular night-time shelter. Shelters and dugouts were constructed underneath roads and houses and even beneath a cemetery. The town's air-raid siren, nicknamed 'Moaning Lizzie', often gave inadequate warning for those who lived some distance from the public shelters, and so many folk dug their own shelters in the back garden.

Another public shelter was provided in the ancient caves behind Oil Mill Barracks. The caves were enormous, perhaps a quarter of a mile long and 15 feet wide, and could shelter up to 10,000 people. Seating and electric lighting were installed and a committee was appointed to organize the place, headed by Dr and Mrs Ord. At the eastern end of the town other caves were made

Sheltering from the bombs in the cellars of the Phoenix Brewery (left) and in the Oil Mill Caves (right).

available and these were placed under a committee led by Mr Licence of the *Dover Chronicle*.

> Visit these caves with me. Outside at the approach would stand a crowd of men smoking – "No Smoking allowed in the Shelters". Inside, brightly illuminated, but still a foggy atmosphere. You would find a bed here made up and the people sleeping, or endeavouring to do so; here a party of children at play; a little further a tea and coffee stall, a concert party, or a four at cards. Special constables on duty keeping order. In the larger caves, Dr and Mrs Ord, controlling a small headquarters, with a staff in case of sickness, had always a kindly word for all. [Coxon]

Air raids on Britain continued throughout 1916 and Dover was bombed by German seaplanes in May, July and August. There was only one visit to Dover by a Zeppelin in 1916, but the threat was ever present.

German Destroyers Sink HMS *Flirt* and HMTS *Queen*

While the war in the air was raging, the Dover Patrol was stretched to its limits in protecting the seaways of the English Channel and the Dover Straits. The greatest and most persistent danger was from submarines, the dreaded U-boats. Rarely did the German Navy risk its warships in direct confrontation with the Royal Navy. Consequently, when German destroyers entered the Channel in force one night in October 1916, the Dover Patrol was ill prepared.

For some days Admiral Bacon, in command of the Dover Patrol, had been receiving reports of increased enemy activity at Ostend, including the arrival of several modern destroyers. On 26 October, with no further intelligence as to the German Navy's intentions, Bacon deployed the

HMS Flirt *was sunk with the loss of most of her crew in October 1916.*

antiquated 30-knotter, HMS *Flirt*, to the eastern end of the Channel under the command of Lieutenant Richard Kellett, supported by a handful of drifters. That same night the Germans sent two divisions of destroyers into the Channel, each of six ships. They divided into two packs and one set out for Dover. *Flirt* saw the enemy vessels but at first took them to be Allied ships on the Dunkirk to Dover crossing. As *Flirt* came across men in the water, a boat was lowered so that the first lieutenant and a seaman could investigate. To aid with the search, and unaware of the danger lurking in the darkness, *Flirt*'s searchlight was turned on. With their targets now illuminated, the enemy ships opened fire on the outnumbered and outgunned *Flirt* and her entourage. *Flirt* sank immediately, together with six of the drifters. The sound of gunfire was heard at Dover and a detachment of Tribals was sent to investigate. HMS *Nubian* arrived and began to pick up survivors but she was then disabled by a torpedo and ran aground. Initial Admiralty reports claimed that two enemy ships had been sunk and that there were nine survivors from *Flirt*. In fact, no enemy ships were sunk, and the only survivors from *Flirt* were the two men who had taken to the ship's boat to rescue men in the sea. A total of forty-five officers and men were lost in the action, among whom was James Doyle, a 16-year-old stoker aboard *Flirt*, who had already seen action at the Battle of Jutland.

The other half of the German destroyer division had headed for Gris-Nez, and the route taken by the Boulogne–Folkestone transport ships.

Although night crossings had been suspended some weeks before because of the danger from submarines, the troopship *Queen* was returning to Folkestone, having earlier delivered her contingent of soldiers in France. The story of *Queen*'s heroic rescue of the crew and passengers of *Amiral Ganteaume* in 1914 has been told in Chapter 2, and since then the ship, still with Captain Carey and crew, had continued her duties without interruption. It was a cruel irony that it was two years to the day since that famous rescue had taken place. With no means of defending herself, *Queen* was quickly overhauled by the enemy ships. Her crew were ordered to the boats, bombs with time fuses were placed, and the ship was cast adrift. Despite explosions tearing through her, the gallant little ship refused to succumb: she drifted for three hours, past Dover and eventually slipped beneath the waves off South Goodwin, where she remains to this day. The explosions were heard in Folkestone and when the *Queen* failed to return on schedule the worst was feared. It was with relief that the watchers later saw Captain Carey and his crew rowing safely into harbour, but it was relief tinged with sadness at the loss of the *Queen*.

1917: All Quiet on the Western Front

The winter of 1916–17 on the Western Front was relatively quiet. No 'big push' but instead plenty of wiring parties in No Man's Land and trench raids. The Battle of the Somme had by no means been decisive, but it had gained a few critical yards for the Allies, and had left the Germans holding a difficult salient. The German High Command had spent the winter planning to shorten and straighten their line and men had been busy building what they called the Siegfried Line, which to the British became known as the infamous Hindenburg Line. The Germans began to vacate their front trenches in February and pulled back to the new defences. Perhaps mistakenly reading this move as a sign of weakness, the Allies were planning a spring offensive – a joint French and British affair, with the Tommies, Canadians and Australians fighting for the northern sector. The Battle of Arras started on Easter Monday, 9 April, and it was at Vimy Ridge that the Canadians earned their immortal reputation. In the air, the RFC was tested to its limits, as the Red Baron and his 'Flying Circus' sent so many British pilots to their deaths, in what became known as 'Bloody April'. For the French the spring offensive was a disaster, and for a time the British were left without an effective ally. General Haig instead looked north, into Belgium, and devised a strategy which, if it succeeded, would isolate the German naval bases at Zeebrugge and Ostend. The Battle of Passchendaele, also known as the Third Battle of Ypres, was the result. The taking of the Messines Ridge near Ypres was the linchpin,

Commander Edward Evans of HMS Broke.

and this was quickly achieved on 7 June, but delay in following up the advantage gave the enemy a chance to dig in. Passchendaele Ridge finally fell in November 1917, but the five-mile advance had cost the British 250,000 casualties and had failed to push through far enough to expose the German submarine bases at Zeebrugge and Ostend, which were causing such destruction to Allied shipping.

Swift and *Broke* Strike Back

The year 1917 was, if anything, worse for Dover than its predecessor. The air raids continued, and with the advent of the Gotha bombers, described in Chapter 4, these became more effective, and so more destructive. The success of the enemy submarine attacks on merchant shipping created the added pressure of acute shortages of almost every commodity from food to clothing. There was precious little from either the war front or at home to raise the spirits, but one event early in the year gave the whole country cause to cheer and created a new national hero, and it happened at Dover.

Commander Edward Evans was already a minor celebrity, having commanded the *Terra Nova* in Scott's expeditions to the Antarctic. He was posted to the Dover Patrol soon after its formation and served there for over three years as a destroyer captain. His own recollection of his duties is one of endless patrols, always hoping for an engagement with enemy warships, which rarely came about: whenever the two combatants met at sea, the German destroyers 'skedaddled'. It was on the night of 20 April 1917 that Evans got his wish. Six modern German destroyers were steaming through the Dover Straits. They may have had no intention of seeking action; perhaps they only wanted the propaganda value of sailing unopposed up the Channel. The modern destroyer HMS *Broke*,

HMS Swift *and HMS* Broke *at anchor in Dover Harbour.*

commanded by Evans, was patrolling in company with HMS *Swift*, under Commander Peck, when the enemy was sighted. Despite the odds, Evans gave immediate orders to close for battle. With shells falling round them the British ships got within torpedo range and sank one ship, while the guns of both British ships put two further German ships out of action. Finally, being too close to use either guns or torpedoes, Evans ordered *Broke* to ram one of the remaining ships. Although sustaining serious damage herself, *Broke* sent her third victim to the bottom. The action had awakened the people of Dover. When they looked out to sea, it was impossible to see what was happening in the dark, but as the British destroyers limped back into port and the news flashed round the harbour, every siren and steam whistle shrieked into life. In an effort to restore some decorum, one harbour officer ordered the din to cease. The response from the trawler crews, with whom Evans was particularly popular, was 'Go to 'ell. It's Teddy.' Within days, headlines across the country were telling the story of *Broke* and *Swift*, and how they defied the odds to keep safe the English Channel.

Summer 1917: the Gotha Raids

Apart from an ineffectual raid by Zeppelins on 16 March, Dover enjoyed a respite from aerial attack for the first half of 1917. However, that summer witnessed the beginning of a bombing campaign against Britain by German Gotha G.IVs, aircraft whose sole purpose was to deliver

This rare photograph of Dover Harbour, taken in 1915 from a German aircraft, has an overlay showing guns and storage tanks, targets for future raids.

destruction on a scale previously unimaginable. After unleashing their devastation on Folkestone on 25 May, the Gothas of Kagohl 3 briefly set course for Dover but, unlike at Folkestone, they were met with a barrage of anti-aircraft fire and veered off without dropping any bombs on the town. To this extent the claim by Berlin, that both towns had been bombed, was incorrect.

Since the Folkestone raid, the Gothas had regularly returned to wreak havoc on Britain. The Thanet towns of Margate and Ramsgate were frequent victims, because of the fact that, although they were of little military significance, they were on the enemy bomber's flight path to London. In late June 1917 command of Kagohl 3 had passed from Hauptmann Brandenburg to Oberstleutnant Hauptmann Rudolph Kleine. Brandenburg's last raid had been on London on 13 June and had caused immense damage and left nearly 600 people killed or injured. For his efforts the Kaiser had awarded Brandenburg the Blue Max, raising him onto the same pedestal as other air aces, such as von Richthofen and Immelman. Kleine had some very large boots to fill.

Raids in July on London and Harwich had been pressed home despite determined fighter and AA resistance and at the cost of several enemy bombers destroyed. The raid on London on 7 July by twenty-one Gothas caused significant damage in the City but, as this was a Sunday, loss of life was less than it might have been. On their inbound journey along the Thames the raiders had gone unchallenged but, as word got round to the various RFC and RNAS airfields, an incredible ninety-five machines took to the air to hunt the enemy. Unfortunately, owing to a lack of co-ordination and to inexperience on the part of many British pilots, this response was not reflected in results.

The outrage following the May attack on Folkestone had led to a rapid improvement in home defences, with improved AA defences and early warnings and, most important, a rapidly improving system of fighter defence provided by the RFC and RNAS. As the 'Gotha Summer' progressed, the tide slowly turned against the raiders, with a number of the bombers being shot down by British fighters or AA guns. Added to the inherent unreliability of the aircraft, the consequent loss of machines and aircrew could not continue.

The Last Daytime Air Raid

The summer of 1917 was the wettest for fifty years. As well as bringing misery to the men in the trenches on the Western Front, it severely hampered Rudolph Kleine's opportunities to mount air raids on Britain. August saw almost constant rain and strong winds. An attempt to launch a raid on 18 August had to be called off, with the loss of a number of aircraft caused by the adverse weather. Had that raid gone ahead, an event in Dover the following day might never have occurred. As a tram full of passengers careened out of control a soldier, Trooper Walter Gunner of the 1st Dragoon Guards, chased after the runaway vehicle and in the process both of his feet were severed by its wheels. For his actions he was awarded the Albert Medal.

Meanwhile, with weather reports showing an improvement, the Kagohl 3 raid was rescheduled for 22 August. Fifteen Gothas took off from Ghent in Belgium just after breakfast time, heading for the Kent coast. Mechanical failures led to five aircraft, including that of Kleine, having to return to base; the remainder pressed on towards London. In the few short weeks since the devastating attack on 25 May 1917, the air defences of Britain had improved dramatically. The first line of defence was the Kentish Knocke Light Vessel, where trained Observers were now stationed, linked with the North Foreland Lookout Station. The enemy was spotted approaching the coast at 9.33 am, with the result that aircraft from RNAS stations at Manston, Eastchurch, Walmer and Dover took to the air to meet the raiders. By the time the Gothas crossed the coast the sixteen fighter aircraft had reached optimum altitudes of 15,000 feet. Beyond the RNAS patrols, a further 120 RFC fighter aircraft had taken to the air to protect the approaches to the capital. The ten Gothas, now

This German photograph shows a Gotha G.IV bomber in its natural element.

under the command of Oberleutnant Walter, made landfall over Thanet and were immediately pounced on by the RNAS aircraft, together with a massive barrage from the AA batteries. One Gotha was hit and spiralled into the sea off Margate, leading Walter to abandon the attack on London and to turn south for Dover: 'I therefore tried, by firing three star flares in quick succession, several times, to instruct the crews to raid Objective No. 3 (Dover). A raid on Dover, in view of the importance of this town to the battle proceeding in Flanders, would have been of the utmost importance.'

As the nine Gothas turned south, another was hit by AA fire and crashed in flames at Margate, killing all three crew. Confusion over the intended target seems to have led a number of Gotha crews to drop their bombs on Ramsgate, but Walter pressed on towards Dover. At approximately 11 am, as the enemy machines came within range, the six AA batteries around Dover opened fire, and the ships in Dover Harbour added to the daunting barrage. The remaining RNAS fighters who were still in pursuit were now joined by RFC machines from Dover, Detling and the Air Park at Lympne. Despite this hot reception, the Gothas managed to unload nine bombs over Dover town and another five in the harbour. The latter caused no damage or casualties, but one bomb which fell on Dover College killed two soldiers. It was after this attack that the decision was made to relocate the college to Leamington Spa for the remainder of the war. Another casualty was teenager Lucy Wall, a barmaid at the Admiral Harvey pub. She was standing in the doorway when the 50kg bomb fell in St Paul's Place, causing a massive explosion which also damaged many nearby properties.

The Gothas then turned eastwards for the journey home. They were still being harried by AA fire and fighter aircraft, and it perhaps gave the defenders some satisfaction to see one of the raiders hit and spiral into the sea just off Dover. The remaining seven Gothas of Kagohl 3, despite continued attacks, managed to reach their base in Flanders just after midday, but they were all riddled with gunfire and, in at least one case, the two gunners were believed to have been killed.

In the few short months since the unopposed attack on Folkestone, the tide had turned against the Gothas. Losses in August had amounted to twenty-two bombers and some forty crew lost. The decision was taken to end daytime raids, but Britain was soon to face the terror of night-time bombing.

Air Raids in the Moonlight

The Germans had always accepted that daytime raids would only be viable until British defences were improved to counter the threat, and the initial prediction that they would become untenable after three months was surprisingly accurate. Plans and training were therefore already under way to switch to night-time raids, and these began almost as soon as the sound of the last daylight bomber had faded from the British skies. The protagonists were still the Gotha G.IV aircraft, but they were joined by a new machine, the Zeppelin-Staaken RVI, otherwise known as the 'Giant'. With seven crewmen and mounting four machine guns and a bomb load of 2,000kg, this bomber outclassed anything that the British could put in the air, and, had not the tide of battle on the Western Front turned against the Germans in the late spring of 1918, its power to devastate British towns might well have brought about a different conclusion to the war.

As navigational aids were rudimentary, the enemy night-time raids could only be launched on a clear night with a good moon. Responsibility for pressing home the attacks against Britain remained with Kleine's Kagohl 3 based in Belgium and, of the precious eighteen Giants which had been manufactured, six were sent to join his squadron.

The first moonlight raid took place less than a fortnight after the last daytime raid. Dover was attacked in six out of the seven raids which took place during September 1917, but with improved early warning systems, casualties were kept to a minimum as the townsfolk made their way to the shelters and caves dotted around the town. Other Kentish towns were not always so lucky: the raid on 4 September left over 130 men dead at Chatham Naval Barracks. In London, people flocked to the underground stations for shelter but, as the moonlight raids continued throughout 1917 and into 1918, the death toll and cost of damage continued to mount.

1918: Hardship on the Home Front

As 1918 dawned no one believed for a moment that it would be the final year of the conflict. The best estimates were that it would continue well into 1919. There was a consensus that, with the Americans having joined the Allies, Germany could not win, but with Russia out of the fight she could concentrate her forces on the Western Front. There was still plenty to fight for before anyone was ready for the peace table. This was clearly demonstrated with the German spring offensive: the Allies were pushed back several miles, back across the Somme battlefields where ground had been so dearly bought in 1916. But the same fate awaited Germany's advance as had stalled the Schlieffen Plan in 1914 – over-extended lines and dogged resistance by the Allies. The advance was halted and slowly the enemy was pushed back.

On the Home Front, 1918 promised to be no less severe than 1917. Food shortages led to the introduction of the Rationing Order in January and over the next few months thousands were prosecuted for breaking the Order. For many the war had gone on long enough. Peace rallies were taking place up and down the country. Where morale had once been maintained by calls for national unity, cracks were now beginning to appear and tougher measures were sometimes called for. In the belief that the moral fabric of society was breaking down, the marked increase in the spread of sexually transmitted diseases was attributed to women having been released from the shackles of domesticity. In March 1918 this led to the passing of Regulation 40D under the Defence of the Realm Act, which made it a criminal offence for a woman with venereal disease to have intercourse with a serviceman, even if he was her husband and he had given her the disease in the first place.

In Dover the need to maintain public support for the war effort was also vigorously enforced. Two related court cases in 1918 demonstrate the particular problems faced, where the warning 'careless talk costs lives' was especially true. The security and safety of the fleet of hospital ships was a matter of great concern for the Dover Patrol, and the declaration by Germany in February 1917 that such ships would henceforth be attacked created the need for even greater vigilance. Germany justified its stance on the grounds that hospital ships were routinely carrying able-bodied troops, a claim strongly denied in Britain. At Dover the use of hospital ships only for the wounded had always been strictly enforced, and it was also forbidden for normal ships to perform any task which might be regarded as medical. However, in view of the new stance by Germany, Dover's white-painted hospital ships highlighted with the emblems of the Red Cross, which would have been such obvious targets, were replaced with camouflaged 'ambulance transports', and provided with light armament for their own defence.

The first court case began with a conversation in a pub in Banbury. A number of locals were discussing the war and the transport of guns and ammunition to France when another man chipped in. This man, it transpired, lived at Sandwich and he declared to folk gathered in the bar, 'Well, if that's all you blokes know about it, it's not much. Would it astonish you if I tell you that I've seen with my own eyes the hospital ships at Dover being loaded with live shell?' Among his audience were two soldiers who reported what they had heard and the man was prosecuted under DORA. Commander Coxon from Dover went up to give evidence, stating that what the man claimed was completely untrue. This man's loose talk cost him six months' hard labour.

The second case followed a newspaper report of a man being convicted for saying that it was common for troops to be transported in hospital ships. The report was read by a constable in the Folkestone Borough Police Force and, amazingly, the constable wrote to the court where the case had been heard with the following claim: 'What Pauer says he was told, every harbour worker in Dover, Folkestone, Calais and Boulogne knows, and sees going on every day since the 18th March [1918], and tons of stores, not only medical. But, nevertheless, you will get a representative from the War Office or Admiralty to swear different, and Pauer goes to the wall. Come and live in Dover and keep your eyes open.' This extraordinary revelation by the Folkestone policeman inevitably led to a prosecution. Commander Coxon, this time with Major McCreery of the RAMC, went to court to 'swear different', but the man changed his plea to guilty at the last minute and his lawyer, Mr Mowl, painted a picture of a devoted public servant who had suffered a moment's indiscretion. The court, expressing its apologies for having to find him guilty, imposed a fine of £5.

The Final Onslaught

As 1918 dawned, Germany remained confident that, with a renewed offensive on the Western Front and continued pressure from sea and air against the British Isles, the Allies could be forced into favourable peace terms. Air raids on London and Kent continued to cause death and damage. At sea, the new mine barrage in the Channel by no means deterred all U-boat commanders. The Dover Patrol could not relax its vigilance.

Major Roderick Dallas was an Australian who had sailed to England at the outbreak of war to join the RNAS. A natural fighter pilot, he had achieved the status of an ace during his time at Dunkirk. He was not pleased that his posting to Dover in early 1918 would take him out of the fray:

R N Aeroplane Station
Dover
26.1.1918

… I have taken over command of Dover Station until I go out to France Dad. I really would much sooner be out there where the real thing is going on, after all one must no longer regard this war as an episode but as life itself and accordingly we must model our careers. There will be great things doing in the spring and I am going to be out there to put every ounce that I can into the thing. We must bear this oily faced brute and the air is the first place that will yield us any result for the effort we must put forth. Well Dad I have every hope that the whole thing will just about pan out this year or early next year … remember me most kindly to all whom I know and tell them my great plan for after the war is to fly from England to Australia and if I get half a chance I am going to do it Dad.

Well goodbye Dad my score is now 30 machines down …

As he had hoped, Major Dallas was posted back to France in the spring. But he never got the chance to fly from England to Australia – he was shot down and killed on 1 June 1918, while involved in a fight against three Fokker Triplanes.

Two weeks after Dallas wrote to his father, Dover was hit again, both from the sea and the air. On 15–16 February six German destroyers launched a raid into the Dover Straits. At the same time, the experimental U-boat UB-57, under the command of Johannes Lohs, entered the Channel. As well as sinking seven drifters and a trawler of the Dover Patrol, the raiders rained shells upon the town. Several people were injured in the midnight attack, including three of the Boorman children, when a shell landed on their home in Cowgate Lane. Their 13-year-old sister Gertrude, whom everyone called 'Girlie', was killed as she lay tucked up in her bed.

The following night the Gotha bombers returned to pound Britain again, dropping the first one-tonne bomb on the Royal Hospital at Chelsea. In the same raid some twenty bombs were unloaded over Dover, but damage was limited and there were no casualties.

There were reports of an attack on Dover on 26 April, this time from a giant long-range gun based at Ostend. The story first broke with a report in the *New York Times*, apparently based on information from Belgian spies working for the British intelligence services. With remarkable detail the report said that three shells landed on Dover, the first sending Shakespeare Cliff tumbling into the sea. Fifty aircraft were said to have taken to the skies to chase off what was thought to be German bombers, but none were located. With the Ministry of Information statement calling the report 'without foundation', it became clear that this was just another wartime rumour.

What was not a rumour was the report that, on 21 April 1918, the German air ace, Baron Manfred von Richthofen, the Red Baron, had finally been brought down and killed over the Western Front. A few short weeks later, on 14 June, the German offensive in France finally came to an end and the final stages of the war began. Between these two events, however, the enemy launched the greatest air raid of the war.

A formation of over forty German bombers took to the air on the evening of 19 May 1918 and set course for the Kent coast, target London. A dozen Gothas had to abandon the mission with the usual engine trouble, but the rest, accompanied by three Giants, pressed home the attack. Ready to meet the foe were the night-fighters of the newly formed Royal Air Force, an amalgamation of the RFC and RNAS. They were, of course, the same pilots, but were now working with clear objectives and in close co-operation with the AA gunners and searchlight crews below. Although the Whit Sunday raid left 49 Londoners dead and 177 injured, it turned into a disaster for Germany as the defenders brought down ten Gothas, killing most of their crews. Three enemy aircraft were shot down over Kent, the fate of one being described in gruesome detail in the *East Kent Gazette*: 'The British airman attacked his opponent so fiercely that the German was forced down to a lower height, and ultimately, to the joy of the onlookers, the Gotha burst into flames, seemed to break in two and came down piecemeal, all aflame. The wrecked machine and the three occupants fell by a farm. Two of the Germans fell into marshy ground and their bodies were deeply embedded in the mud. The third man's head struck a wall and was shattered like an eggshell. All three bodies were removed to a local aviation establishment. The fall of the burning Gotha was seen for miles around.'

As the raiders ran the gauntlet of fire, one of them flew over Dover and, before heading out to sea for the flight home, dropped a bomb which fell harmlessly in a farmer's field at St Margaret's just east of Dover; it was to be the very last bomb dropped on British soil during the Great War, and was the spot chosen to site the memorial to the Dover Patrol.

The Sacrifice of HMS *Glatton*

The greatest single loss of life in Dover during the Great War was suffered not at the hands of the enemy but on the direct orders of Admiral Keyes, the commander of the Dover Patrol, and it occurred within two months of the end of the war.

HMS *Glatton* was a new Gorgon-class monitor and had just arrived at Dover. On 16 September 1918, *Glatton* was moored inside the harbour being prepared for sea. Her magazines were full of ammunition and explosives, and the stokers were feeding the boilers ready for the order to cast off. At 6.15 pm there was a sudden explosion amidships which quickly developed into a fierce fire. People living along the harbour front came rushing out of their homes and they were soon joined by more townsfolk trying to get a glimpse of the unfolding disaster. The fire took a firm grip and it quickly became clear that the ship's magazines were at risk of going up and, with the ammunition ship *Gransha* berthed nearby, the consequences could have spelled destruction not only for the harbour and ships, but also for much of the town. Such was the danger that the Mayor sounded the town's air-raid siren.

Attempts by the tug *Lady Brassey* to put out the fire were unsuccessful. For Admiral Keyes time and options were running out. As the police, assisted by troops with bayonets fixed, began evacuating people from their homes and putting up barriers to keep them away from the danger area, Keyes and another officer clambered from *Lady Brassey* onto the deck of *Glatton*. They managed to reach the controls to flood the forward magazines, but were beaten back by fire from the main deck, where the aft flooding controls were located. The fire had now been raging for over an hour and it was spreading. A number of men had escaped the inferno, but many were still aboard, trapped below decks, waiting for rescue.

Keyes, accepting that he now had only one option left, to sink *Glatton*,

The hull of HMS Glatton, *which was sunk in Dover Harbour in 1918 on the orders of Roger Keyes with great loss of life.*

boarded the destroyer HMS *Cossack* and gave the order for an 18-inch torpedo to be fired. Being fired from point-blank range, the torpedo failed to explode, and a second attempt also failed to sink the stricken ship. Keyes then boarded the destroyer *Myngs* and ordered two torpedoes to be fired simultaneously. They detonated on her starboard side just below the water line and *Glatton* succumbed and keeled over, instantly extinguishing the flames. The men still on board had no chance of escape; those not killed by the explosion were drowned. Among the individual acts of heroism that day, as men tried often in vain to save their comrades, was that of Edward Atkinson. He was the ship's surgeon and, despite being blinded and burned, he managed to rescue several men before jumping clear of the stricken vessel. Atkinson was awarded the Albert Medal.

Over the following days sections of hull were removed and the bodies of the victims were recovered. Later a memorial service was held on the upturned hull. A total of ninety-eight men, most of them stokers and mechanics, had died either at the time or later from their injuries. As for HMS *Glatton*, the Admiralty could find no one to salvage her, and she remained in the harbour until, in 1925, Captain John Iron offered to undertake the task. Her remains joined the scrapyard at the eastern end of the harbour, which for many years was the final resting place of a number of ships, until Dover Harbour Board cleared the site in the mid-1960s to make way for the Eastern Docks.

Constancy.

'Tis sweet to be remembered,
And a pleasant thing to find,
That though you may be absent,
You still are kept in mind.

Postcard Home

Dover 17th September 1918
Dear Sweetheart,
Just a line before I set sail to let you know I am in the best of health. I hope this card finds you the same. So long Dear for the present.

Your loving sweetheart, Jim
xxxxxxxxxx

Does not this one make you think Dear of the time that has just passed?

Target Dover. A German propaganda illustration of a full scale air raid on Dover Harbour.

Chapter 7

The Dover Patrol and the Zeebrugge Raid

The Dover Patrol

Our purpose here is to give a broad view of the activities of the Dover Patrol during the Great War, focusing on some of the less well-known events and personalities. The Kent coast has for centuries been a focus for British merchant and naval shipping, although the harbour at Dover was never a favoured spot because of the difficult tides and the problem of silting. During the early years of the twentieth century, the Admiralty embarked upon a programme to develop Dover Harbour as a base for the Royal Navy. Many millions of pounds were spent in creating the outer harbour by extending the eastern and western arms and enclosing it with the outer harbour wall. In 1909 the final touches were completed when the Prince of Wales opened the new pier which bore his name. However, despite its size and the expense of construction, the new harbour was not considered suitable for the Grand Fleet, which remained safely tucked away at Scapa Flow. Instead, Dover became home to the Sixth Destroyer Flotilla. On 13 October 1914 Rear-Admiral Horace Hood was put in command at Dover, and his early grasp of what was happening in Belgium led to the first campaigns by what became known as the Dover Patrol. In an attempt to impede German entrenchment on the Belgian coast, Hood sent his ships to bombard the enemy positions. As well as his destroyers, the admiral had three monitors, essentially floating gun platforms, from which 6-inch shells were hurled ashore. High sand dunes meant that it was impossible to aim the guns or to know what effect they were having. It was later found that, although little material damage was caused, the constant shelling caused disruption and consternation among the German army. Early in 1915 Hood was reassigned to command cruisers off the Irish coast and Admiral Sir Reginald Bacon was appointed to command at Dover.

Bacon had previously designed and overseen the deployment in France of 15-inch howitzers. He brought with him to Dover an imaginative mind and endless energy, and during his tenure the Patrol developed into a massive organization. There were well over 300 ships and vessels of every description

– monitors and mine layers, destroyers and drifters, submarines, trawlers and coastal motor boats. In addition to the seagoing force there was the airborne element of a seaplane base, an RNAS aircraft station, and a separate airship station. To repair, service and refuel all the ships of the Patrol, plus the submarines and seaplanes, and maintain the harbour structures and defences required a comprehensive engineering facility. Initially, the dockyard work was carried out in a few pre-war huts, but new workshops for engineering and electrical work were constructed in 1915. The workshops of the Dover Engineering Company, the South-Eastern & Chatham Railway and Palmers Sheet Metal Works were all requisitioned by the Admiralty, and naval mechanics were supplemented by civilian workers. To maintain the combat vessels, the harbour was a constant hive of activity, with tugs, colliers, oilers and water tankers all ensuring that their charges were ready to return to sea without delay.

Two tugs belonging to Dover Harbour Board, the *Lady Brassey* and the *Lady Crundall*, were taken over by the Admiralty and served throughout the war. They came under the command of the aptly named Captain John Iron, the Dover Harbourmaster. Iron's grandfather had been a Cinque Ports Pilot from 1808 until 1832, when he became Harbourmaster at Dover, being followed by his son, and then by John. Such vast experience was not wasted on Admiral Bacon, who appointed Captain Iron as his Chief Salvage Officer and no better person could have been chosen. Well over a hundred naval and merchant ships were salvaged by Iron and his tugs during the war.

Motor launches in Dover Harbour.

As the war progressed the operations of the Dover Patrol developed both to counter new threats and, where possible, to contribute to the war effort in France and Flanders. In the latter category, the greatest contribution was made by the monitors. These were ships designed as floating gun platforms. From the 6-inch guns first used by Hood, the armament increased to 12-inch and then 15-inch. Their effectiveness was demonstrated by the fact that the Germans had to install more and larger guns along the Belgian coast to hit back at the monitors.

One example of the monitors in action will demonstrate their value and, incidentally, tells the story of a remarkable sailor. As Sir John French was planning the Battle of Loos, the 'big push' which was to see the British army break through the German trenches in northern France, he sought the aid of Admiral Bacon and the Dover Patrol. It was agreed that a diversion would be created along the Belgian coast, feigning a seaborne landing. In preparation for the 'invasion' on 24 September 1915, the evening before the real battle began, the monitors *Prince Eugene* and *General Craufford*, with five destroyers, two minesweepers, the yacht HMS *Sanda* and a division of drifters, set off to bombard Zeebrugge. The next morning Admiral Bacon led the remainder of the 12-inch monitors and the 15-inch *Marshal Ney* to a position off Middelkerke. The bombardment by both divisions began at 7 am. At 9 am the German guns began to reply and almost immediately hit and sank the *Sanda*. The drifter *Fearless* immediately went to save the crew, but all of her executive officers, including her skipper, were lost. The operation continued for the next few days, with *Sir John Moore* also joining the attack.

Regarding the loss of the *Sanda*, it might well be asked what a yacht was

HMS Sir John Moore. *The monitors were essentially floating gun platforms used to pound German positions in Belgium.*

Officers of HMS Sir John Moore.

doing in the midst of a naval bombardment of the enemy coast. She was attached to the drifter patrols and, almost certainly, her role was to act as a rescue boat. Her skipper was Lieutenant Commander Henry Gartside-Tipping, who had come out of retirement to take command of the *Sanda*. At sixty-seven years of age he was the oldest serving officer in the Royal Navy and, it is believed, the oldest serving casualty of the Great War. On the day before his fateful last voyage, Gartside-Tipping had been introduced to the King, who had come to Dover to inspect the Dover Patrol. In his memory a motor boat, named the *Henry Gartside-Tipping*, was donated by his family to the Missions for Seamen in Dover in June 1916. The ceremony took place on the beach close to the clock tower, attended by a choir, a drum and fife band, and a host of VIPs. The story does not quite end there, as Henry's widow, Mary, became a casualty of war in 1917. After her husband's death she worked for nearly a year at the Munitions Workers' Canteen, Woolwich, and in January 1917 joined the Women's Emergency Corps for service in the war zone in France, where she was shot by a soldier whose mind was disordered. Mary was awarded the Croix de Guerre and given a full military funeral.

One of the most important tasks of the Dover Patrol was to shepherd the troop and supply ships between Dover and Folkestone and the French ports.

As previously stated, these ships were the lifeline of Britain's war effort on the Western Front. Every crossing had to be guarded and a constant search-and-destroy screen had to be maintained for enemy submarines and minefields. To achieve these objectives the Patrol used a combination of strategies. The troopship convoys were escorted by the destroyers, while overhead there would either be kite balloons tethered to the patrolling armed trawlers or the self-propelled airships.

The Airships

The airships were based at the RNAS station at Capel le Ferne, a village sitting on top of the cliffs between Dover and Folkestone. There was a certain irony in the fact that the first airships employed were the German Parseval models. The British programme of airship construction had been effectively abandoned after early failures. In command at Capel le Ferne was Lieutenant Commander Alexander Cunningham. During his twelve-hour flights along the Kent coast, Cunningham was devising plans for an improved airship, leading to the development of the SS-Zero, an 80-foot-long non-rigid ship with a pusher propeller and self-start engine. One hundred and twenty-five Submarine Scout airships were built and used for

Airships from RNAS Capel le Ferne worked with ships to spot and attack German U-boats in the Channel.

anti-submarine patrols around the British coast throughout the war. Cunningham is also credited with another, slightly more sublime, contribution to airship development: as he was carrying out one of his weekly inspections at Capel he tapped an airship and, it is said, the sound it made was 'blimp', and that became the popular name by which airships were known.

Some years after the war, an article appeared in the *Folkestone Herald*, written by a veteran of RNAS Capel le Ferne, recalling events there:

> A special recruiting campaign locally resulted in a good number of Folkestone young men joining the RNAS service at Capel. Just before I arrived there one of the earliest blimps, known as 'Silver Queen', went up in flames after hitting some overhead wires, and as a precaution against further disasters of that kind wires were put underground. One blimp was lost in the Warren. The envelopes of these ships were divided into three sections, the centre containing hydrogen gas and the stern and nose ends, air, which was fed through a duct at the back of the propeller which was driven by a single motor. With the engine failing the air supply failed as well. Slowly each end of the blimp became deflated and it eventually flopped rather ungracefully to earth in the Warren. On another occasion four blimps

The Submarine Scout class of airship was developed at Capel.

were caught in a sudden sea mist. But all except one got back to Capel safely. The odd one made a landfall in a meadow opposite the Valiant Sailor public house where two of Mr Aird's farm hands managed to secure it until our arrival. We 'walked' the airship back to Capel, across fields and lanes.

In addition to the rigid airships based at Capel, there was a fleet of kite balloons. These were tethered to patrol ships and towed across the Channel, from where observers could spot submarines. To cater for the sometimes unpredictable flying characteristics of balloons and airships, a number of out-stations were provided for them. One of these was situated in Hythe at the end of Range Road, with the Green being used as a recovery ground (there is still a large iron tethering ring to be found sunk in concrete on the Green, used for securing the kite balloons).

It is difficult to measure the contribution of the airships. Their principal duty was to work with the destroyers on the cross-channel troopship crossings, spotting for submarines and, when opportunity arose, to attack them with bombs. Only one actual sinking of a submarine by airship was ever claimed with any confidence, although several were attacked. Their real contribution was that of deterrence – keeping the U-boats submerged and preventing them from launching torpedoes. Certainly the Germans knew the value of the airships, because they specifically attacked Capel Airship Station on at least two occasions, once from the sea and once from the air. Another measure of the importance of Capel was that the Belgian painter, Louis Raemaekers, renowned for his graphic anti-German pictures, painted two pictures of the station. Intended for use on postcards, one of the paintings is held by the Science Museum in London, the other by the authors, and is reproduced on the back cover.

As well as the airships and kite balloons, there were the aircraft of the RNAS, which came under the command of the Dover Patrol. Locally, they had airfields at Guston in Dover and at Walmer, but also used the Airship Station at Capel. RNAS seaplanes also flew from Dover and Walmer.

The Drifters and Trawlers

While much of the work of the Dover Patrol was visible to the casual observer, with the airships and seaplanes coming and going, and destroyers, trawlers and other vessels carrying out their patrol and escort duties, a great deal was unseen. The greatest threat to the security of the English Channel was from German U-boats and, to counter these, a complex underwater system of defence was created.

A drifter of the Dover Patrol laying anti-submarine nets.

Fleets of drifters and trawlers from the British fishing fleets, drawn principally from Humberside and the Kent coast, complete with their crews, were drafted into the Dover Patrol to help with anti-submarine work. The drifter crews were under the charge of naval officers and subject, in theory at least, to Royal Navy discipline. The First Lieutenant of the Drifter Patrol, Captain George Venn, soon realized that the fishermen were not going to be amenable to strict naval etiquette, calling the officer in charge, Captain Bowring, 'Dick', and wearing their uniforms as though they had come from a pawnbroker's shop. In charge of discipline was the Master-at-Arms, Joseph Henry Bailey, who, with Charles Lightoller, a destroyer captain with the Dover Patrol, shared the distinction of being a survivor of the *Titanic* disaster of 1912.

During 1915 a plan was conceived to create a barrage of steel nets across the Channel between Folkestone and Gris-Nez. Strong tides proved too much for these early obstacles, with the friction and pressures shearing through the metal chains. Another net barrage laid between the Goodwins and the French coast was more successful. These nets were suspended in the water from floats, the idea being that enemy submarines, especially those trying to lay mines in the Channel, would become entangled in the nets, the tell-tale bobbing floats would bring ships of the Dover Patrol to the scene,

Left: Captain F Bird of the Drifter Patrol aboard his 'flagship', the East Briton.
Right: drifters in Dover Harbour.

and the U-boat would be despatched with gunfire or depth charges. The nets were fired from the drifters, and thereafter they would be watched and checked for damage. It was hard, relentless work and sometimes dangerous: if a rogue mine had become caught up in the nets, the task of recovery could easily end in disaster. On occasions the drifters accompanied the monitors as they set out to bombard Zeebrugge and Ostend, their job being to set nets around the monitors to prevent submarine attacks. This, of course, put the unarmed drifters in the line of fire as the German shore batteries exchanged shells with the monitors. It was on such a mission that the *Great Heart* was lost on 24 September 1916, which went down with Skipper William Donaldson and seven crewmen.

The trawlers of the Dover Patrol numbered sixty-six and they performed three principal roles: patrolling, minesweeping and mine laying. Armed with a 6-pounder high-angle gun, a 7.5-inch howitzer and depth charges, and equipped with hydrophones and wireless, these handy vessels were avoided like the plague by enemy submarines. Talking of the plague recalls a story about an incident involving a Dover trawler. An unwell crew member was diagnosed by the doctor as having rheumatism and was ordered to hospital. The doctor told the captain to radio for an ambulance to meet the boat to take the man to hospital. The hospital waited for the man to arrive but, when he did not, the somewhat irate doctor returned to the trawler to find out where the patient was. The captain told him, 'Well, we tried to send him ashore, but a sergeant of police and a constable hailed us and said that on no account was he to be landed, or we'd be fined hundreds of pounds, so we kept him on board.' Mystified, the doctor asked whether the message had been sent as he had instructed, to which the captain replied, 'Yes we did, but neither me nor the signalman knew how to spell rheumatism, so we called it smallpox.'

In their role as patrol vessels, the trawlers carried out escort duties, leading cross-channel convoys through the net barrages and minefields, and they were often first on the scene to carry out rescue duties, such being the case when both the P&O *Maloja* and the hospital ship *Anglia* were attacked, and they also saved the crews of eighteen British aircraft which ditched into the sea. As minesweepers, the trawlers would act in pairs with a steel wire trailing between them, which would either sever the mines from their anchors or, if the wire hit a horn on the mine, detonate it. This was dangerous work and accounted for many of the twenty-five trawlers lost during the war.

Initially only six of the trawlers were equipped for mine-laying duties, but this number was doubled late in 1917. During the early years of the war, several methods of deploying mines in the Channel were tried, but a combination of unreliability and the vagaries of the tides rendered them less than wholly effective. It was a standing joke among the U-boat crews that British mines never worked. All that changed at the end of 1917 when, together with the introduction of the more reliable Type H2 mine (copied from a German design), the Mining School came up with a better method of securing them to the seabed. The plan was to use nets at the more shallow depths, below which would be mines at different depths. Several thousand mines were laid and the dual defences of the Dover and Folkestone Barrages were ready for duty. It was not long before this dangerous and time-consuming operation was paying dividends. The first victim was UB-56, which struck a mine in the Dover Straits on 19 December 1917 and sank with the loss of all thirty-seven crew. Between then and 29 August 1918 another ten U-boats were lost to mines in the Channel, together with the lives of 333 German submariners.

> See hidden in the muddy tide 'twixt Folkestone and Grisnez,
> Mines in their thousand, floating, bar the underwater way.
> Blood-red the mines are painted, and the water black as jet –
> Both *Rouge et Noir* assembled for the Dover Straits Roulette.
>
> (Bacon, *The Dover Patrol*)

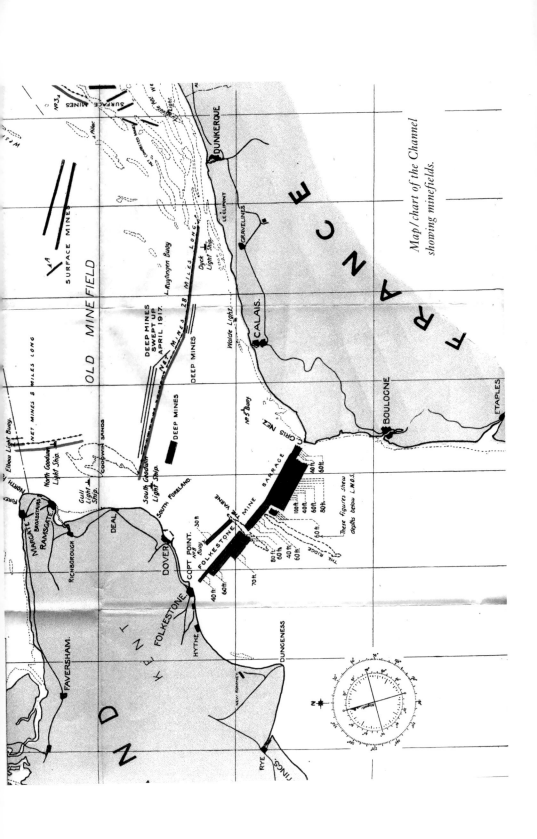

Map/chart of the Channel
showing minefields.

A C-class British submarine in Dover Harbour.

Reginald Bacon was replaced at Dover by Vice-Admiral Roger Keyes in January 1918 (he was knighted in April that year). There were many, including most of the men and officers of the Dover Patrol, who believed that Bacon had been poorly treated, and Keyes was given a cool reception. 'How he shook us all up when he got there,' complained one sailor; 'we always used to be able to count on Sundays in port. But all that changed as soon as Sir Roger came!' Keyes, and the Admiralty, had become concerned that an air of complacency had crept over the Patrol's anti-submarine strategy, and Keyes insisted on a far more aggressive role by his warships. He reversed Bacon's policy of not illuminating the Channel at night. As Winston Churchill later wrote, 'He had soon redoubled the patrols; and by night the barrage from end to end became as light as Piccadilly.'

We have given an outline of the work of some of the less belligerent elements of the Dover Patrol. They are sometimes overlooked in favour of the more conventional fighting vessels: the cruisers, destroyers, submarines and torpedo boats. We should, however, remember the words of Joseph Conrad: 'But that which in the instance kept the German forces from breaking disastrously on any dark night into the Channel and jeopardising the very foundations of our resisting power, were not the wonderfully planned and executed defences of nets and mines, but the inimitable hearts of the men of the Dover Patrol.'

The Raid on Zeebrugge

Every child knows the story of Zeebrugge, the one naval exploit of the war that moved and still moves the imagination of the Nation. Sir Roger Keyes, the Admiral who directed the attack, had the unmistakable Nelson Touch.

This is how Lloyd George, the British wartime Prime Minister, described the raid on Zeebrugge in his memoirs. The raid was planned and launched from Dover, and took place on St George's Day, 1918. There is still doubt about the material impact of the raid, but of its audacity and morale-boosting value, and the bravery of those who took part, there is none.

As 1918 dawned and the Allies prepared themselves for yet another year of war, the outlook was bleak. In the corridors of Whitehall it was quietly hoped that, with the Americans entering the war, victory might be achieved some time in 1919. On the home front, the Christmas of 1917 was celebrated with whatever could be scraped together after queuing at the shops for hours. For all but the wealthy, the need to send the best of the nation's dwindling food supplies to the fighting men, together with the loss of so much food at the hands of the marauding U-boats, meant that there would be little on the table. The government was putting the finishing touches to plans for general rationing, to be introduced in January 1918.

The Battle of Passchendaele in July 1917 should have seen the army dislodge the Belgian ports from enemy control. It was from those ports, particularly Zeebrugge, that their submarines set off on their missions to sink the merchant ships which brought the supplies to beleaguered Britain from America and the Empire. Despite the loss of 100,000 men, the summer offensive, which had dragged on into the autumn, had achieved only limited success, and the German U-boats still set out from their Belgian lairs with impunity.

On 1 January 1918 command of the Dover Patrol was handed over to Vice-Admiral Roger Keyes. Keyes had some interesting connections with the Kent coast. During his early years in the navy, his parents had lived at Shorncliffe Lodge in Sandgate and he had spent time there when on leave. He often visited Shorncliffe army camp and enjoyed playing polo with the cavalry officers there. But perhaps the most curious connection was that a distant ancestor, Richard Keyes, had built Sandgate Castle for Henry VIII, and then became its first Captain, defending the Kent coast from the country's enemies. It was fitting that, nearly 400 years later, another Keyes had again taken up the mantle.

The Challenge

Zeebrugge was the home of the dreaded U-boats of II Flotille, Unterzeebootflotille Flandern, and of the seaplanes of Seeflugstation Flandern, together with torpedo boats and destroyers of the Flotilla Flandern. Being a mere 70 miles from the British coast, with easy access to the North Sea, and sitting on the doorstep of the Channel, Zeebrugge was a thorn in the side of the British Admiralty. It was the Dover Patrol that had the job of disrupting what was effectively a guerrilla force which, left unchecked, could plunder the cross-channel ships taking men and materials to France. The Germans had taken possession of the West Flanders coastline in October 1914 and wasted no time in fortifying the coast and harbours. Zeebrugge Harbour was connected via a navigable canal to Bruges and it was here that the Germans had built submarine pens, docks and workshops, all with impregnable concrete roofs. Many U-boat raids had set out from Zeebrugge. The first had taken place on 11 November 1914: U-12 had only arrived at Zeebrugge two days earlier and, on her first hunt, came across HMS *Niger*, a torpedo-gunboat, lying off Deal. A torpedo sent *Niger* to the bottom but, according to an Admiralty statement, 'All the officers and 77 of the men were saved; two of the men are severely and two slightly injured. It is thought there was no loss of life.'

But the U-boats by no means had it all their own way – the hunters could very quickly become the hunted. U-8 suffered such a fate on 4 March 1915 as she set off to hunt in the Dover Straits. Having become entangled in the anti-submarine nets of the Dover barrage, like a fly in a spider's web, the more she struggled the more the buoys bobbed, alerting the Dover Patrol destroyers, HMS *Maori* and *Ghurka*. As the ships closed in, the crew of U-8 abandoned the doomed vessel and looked on as the submarine was sent to the bottom.

It was also from Zeebrugge that, on 10 March 1915, one of Germany's U-boat aces, Kapitanleutnant Otto von Weddigen set out in boat U-29. He had achieved fame when, on 22 September 1914, he torpedoed and sank three British cruisers, HMS *Aboukir*, *Cressy* and *Hogue*. The fact that the British ships were obsolete, and secretly called the 'live bait squadron', did nothing to lessen the impact of such losses inflicted by a solitary U-boat. The news of the losses was felt nowhere more acutely than in Dover, home of at least ten of the sailors who perished that day. Weddigen was decorated by the Kaiser with the Pour le Mérite, the Blue Max, but his success was short-lived: on 18 March 1915 U-29 was rammed by HMS *Dreadnought* and Weddigen went down with the rest of his crew.

There was no doubt that to put Zeebrugge and the canal out of action would deal a serious blow to enemy naval activities. As early as 4 January 1915 Admiral Sir Arthur Wilson, First Lord of the Admiralty, had sent a minute to Winston Churchill pointing out the need to block the canal. Since 1916 a number of schemes had been put forward, but none had been acceptable to the Admiralty. Before an attacking force even reached Zeebrugge, it had to run the gauntlet of minefields, shore guns (of which there were 225 along this stretch of coast), engagement by German surface and submarine craft, and bombardment from the air. If these were all safely negotiated, the harbour itself was defended by shore batteries with 5.9-inch guns and the Mole, which extended for nearly two miles into the sea, complete with a railway and gun emplacements, and a permanent garrison of a thousand men (though German sources claim the number was less than 100). Added to this was the fact that there were likely to be torpedo boats and destroyers moored in the harbour, which would add their firepower to the fixed guns in the event of an attack. Having avoided all of these obstacles, the attacking force next had to enter the inner harbour, still under fire, and reach the canal entrance, which was only possible through a boom constructed of nets and barges. Finally, there was the weather: without exactly the right conditions, of moon, sea state and wind, the enterprise could not succeed, and any attempt made in the wrong conditions would turn a highly risky business into a suicide mission.

The Plan

Put simply, the plan was to land an assault force on the Mole, blow up the viaduct and, in the confusion caused by these attacks, three blockships could enter Zeebrugge Harbour unmolested and be sunk in the mouth of the canal. Split-second timing would be needed.

The mouth of the canal as it entered Zeebrugge Harbour was wide enough and deep enough for German craft, but only just. The plan was to block the canal, thus rendering all enemy vessels then at Bruges effectively landlocked, and preventing others from seeking safe haven there. The most effective way of blocking this channel was to sink blockships in it, preferably across the deepest section of the canal, so that nothing could sail past or over the obstacle. Keyes gave one of his officers the task of scouring British docks and harbours for suitable candidates, bearing in mind that the operation was clothed in utmost secrecy so the real purpose for asking for the ships could not be disclosed, nor could the fact that they would not be returned! Three old light cruisers were found, HMS *Thetis*, *Intrepid* and *Iphigenia*. (Two others, *Brilliant* and *Sirius*, were also commandeered for the operation at Ostend.) The crews of the blockships had to be volunteers. Keyes felt that their mission was so dangerous that men could not be ordered to undertake the task. To minimize the casualties, the crews would be kept to the bare minimum, with passage crews being removed before the final run-in to the canal entrance, leaving the volunteer crew of about sixty men to undertake the most hazardous part of the trip. There had already been something of a minor mutiny about this arrangement, when several crew of *Intrepid* had asked to see the captain and their spokesman had announced, 'Well Sir, me and my mates understands how some of the crew have got to leave the ship on the way to Zeebryuggy. The jaunty [master-at-arms] says it's us lot and we ain't a-goin' to leave.'

Next came the question: how to get the blockships into position without them being sunk by the defenders long before they had even entered the harbour? Clearly, the enemy would need to be distracted or his guns put out of action, or both. To achieve these objectives a series of schemes was devised. It was inventive and complex and would require split-second timing to be successful. The first element was to get the blockships safely to their destination. Negotiating the rapidly moving shoals and enemy minefields at night and without lights would require top-class navigators. As the armada approached the enemy coast and ran in towards the Zeebrugge guns they would need to be protected somehow. To help to solve a number of these problems the services of a remarkable man were enlisted. Wing Commander Frank Brock, RNAS, had already made a contribution to the work of the Dover Patrol by inventing the Dover Flare, which turned the Straits at night 'from end to end as bright as Piccadilly'.

Frank Arthur Brock was born in 1884 into the family of the famous firework manufacturers, C T Brock & Co. After attending Dulwich College, where he managed to blow up a stove in his form room, he entered the family business and developed his inventive talents, especially for anything connected with pyrotechnics. At the outbreak of war Brock was commissioned into the Royal Artillery but soon transferred to the RNAS, though his flying days were curtailed when his particular skills were recognized. He became a member of the Admiralty Board of Inventions and Research, where, as well as the Dover Flare, he developed the Brock Incendiary Bullet for use against Zeppelins.

On arrival at Dover in early 1918, Brock was briefed on the plan to attack Zeebrugge, and the use of smokescreens by the attacking vessels was explained. The key drawback of the current method of creating a smokescreen was that it also created a huge flame which, of course, would defeat the object as the German gunners would simply fire at that.

With sixty men working under him in a factory in Dover, Brock soon came up with the solution. He called it 'artificial fog', a chemical mixture which was injected directly under pressure into the hot exhausts of motor torpedo boats and other small craft or the hot interior surface of the funnels of destroyers. The larger ships each had welded iron contraptions, in the region of 10 feet in height, into which were fed solid cakes of phosphide of calcium. Dropped into a bucket-like container full of water, the resulting smoke and flames roared up a chimney and were dispersed by a windmill arrangement. One of the ingredients for the brew being concocted by Brock was saxin, which was a popular substitute for sugar. He required so much that, with the blessing of the War Cabinet, all supplies in March and April were diverted to the factory in Dover. The reason for the nation's forced dependence on unsweetened tea was, of course, kept secret. During the trials for the smokescreen, chaos was said to have been caused in the Dover Straits when the smoke lingered for three days, and captains of merchant ships sent in complaints to the weathermen, who had mentioned nothing of fog in their forecasts. Brock's contribution to the Zeebrugge Raid was not limited to his fog. One difficulty the attacking force would face would be navigation – finding its way in the dark into enemy waters. Buoys could be useful, but if they were laid too long before the operation the Germans would spot them, and it would take too long on the night to light and lower the buoys currently in use. Brock needed no more than twenty-four hours to design and manufacture the answer – buoys which lit up as soon as they were thrown into the water.

Another part of the plan was to put the German guns on the Mole out of action. A direct attack on the Mole would have the additional benefit of diverting attention away from the blockships making their way into the harbour. The attack would have to be launched against the external face of the Mole, whose height above sea level, depending on the state of the tide, was between 29 and 44 feet. This was to be the task of HMS *Vindictive* and her two chaperones, *Iris* and *Daffodil*. *Vindictive*, another light cruiser, had originally been earmarked for the same ignoble end as the other blockships, but her reprieve meant that her fighting days were far from over. First she had to be made ready for the job ahead, with a special deck to which eighteen gangways were fixed which, on reaching the Mole, would be lowered onto the top of the parapet for the assault parties to cross. As she would be going in under fire, the ship was provided with additional weaponry, including pom-poms, a Lewis gun high in the foretop, trench mortars, machine guns and two large flame-throwers specially designed by Wing Commander Brock.

Unnecessary rigging and masts were removed and all controls were

The Mersey ferries, Iris *and* Daffodil, *which took part in the Zeebrugge raid.*

triplicated. As well as their crews, dispersed throughout *Vindictive, Daffodil* and *Iris* would be the Mole storming parties of 200 sailors and 400 men from the 4th Battalion Royal Marines Light Infantry. Their task would be to secure the Mole and destroy the enemy guns and, while there, do as much general damage as they could. The specially installed guns on *Vindictive,* designed to give her defensive capability in the close confines of the expected firefight at the Mole, were to be manned by men of the Royal Marines Artillery.

Iris and *Daffodil* were tough little ferries from the River Mersey. They were chosen to carry the rest of the storming parties, bearing in mind that *Vindictive* was likely to come under heavy fire and suffer the loss of men before they even had a chance to clamber across to the Mole. Additionally, *Daffodil* was to act as a tugboat for *Vindictive,* pushing the latter hard against the Mole wall while seamen secured her by use of grapnels. Any doubts about the ability of these unlikely warriors were dispelled when they arrived at Dover, one with her anti–submarine escort in tow. Both vessels were given naval crews and allowed to adopt the title HMS.

Assuming HMS *Vindictive* reached her goal and disgorged the storming parties, there remained the problem of how to prevent reinforcements coming to the aid of the German troops caught on the Mole. There were the barracks of the Marinekorps, plus men from the artillery and the seaplane station, who could dash along the Mole in a matter of minutes. The answer was to simply cut off the Mole from the shore. To enable tidal flow to be

HMS Restless, *one of the few modern destroyers in the Dover Patrol.*

maintained, one section of the Mole was not solid concrete but a viaduct made of a lattice-work of timber and metal. Two British submarines would be loaded with high explosives and, sailing with skeleton crews, ram the viaduct, where timed fuses would be set and the crews make a hasty getaway in small powered dinghies. The chances of survival for these submarine crews were very slim.

Having taken care of the principal vessels – the blockships, *Vindictive, Iris* and *Daffodil,* and the submarines – there was the rest of the armada to consider. These included monitors to bombard the coast, destroyers, and a host of motor launches and fast motor boats. The smaller craft would have plenty to do: they would lead the blockships into the harbour and attack any enemy ship found there; they would lay down the smokescreen all along the coast; and they would take the leading role in rescue and recovery. In all, 162 vessels were directly employed in the operation.

'St George for England': the Attack

In deciding on a date for the attack, Admiral Keyes had set a number of criteria: the tides, the wind and the moon all had to be just right. High tide was necessary to enable the blockships to steam into the mouth of the canal, the winds had to be off the sea so that the all-important smokescreens would waft onshore and hide the armada from the German batteries, and it had to

The crew of another modern destroyer, HMS Trident, *pictured in Dover Harbour.* Trident *took part in the Zeebrugge raid.*

be a moonless night for the same reason. There was a window of opportunity on 11 April but, having set out, the convoy had to turn back as it reached the point of no return, because the wind shifted and started to blow off the land. The disappointment felt by everyone was made worse by an Admiralty decision to scrap the whole affair. After the weeks of training the men were discharged and returned to their original ships and units. But Keyes was not a man to give up. Not only was he acutely aware that the plan offered a chance of dealing a serious blow to German naval activities, but he also knew that the outcome of the war at that moment hung in the balance. On the Western Front, the German offensive was gaining ground, pushing the Allies back over ground which had been bought at such cost over two years before. The situation was desperate and on 11 April, the day of the abortive raid on Zeebrugge, Sir Douglas Haig had issued his famous 'To the last man' Order of the Day which left his men, and the nation, in no doubt about the danger: 'With our backs to the wall, and believing in the justice of our cause, each one of us must fight on to the end. The safety of our homes and the freedom of mankind depend alike upon the conduct of each one of us at this critical moment.' Keyes believed that he and his men could still play their part in this pivotal moment in history and he proposed to the Admiralty that the attack could still go ahead with one key change to the original plan – it could take place even on a moonlit night. This was a high-risk strategy, but he persuaded the First Sea Lord that it could be pulled off – though, as he later recalled, 'Some of my staff were doubtful of my wisdom, but I had a feeling that our hour had come.'

The hour did come on 22 April and at 5 pm Admiral Keyes hoisted his flag on the destroyer HMS *Warwick*, and left Dover Harbour for the rendezvous point with the rest of the armada. As he had left, his wife Eva reminded him that the next day would be St George's Day and urged him to use 'St George for England!' as his battle-cry, and that is the signal he sent by semaphore to his fleet as they set sail. As the ships set out in three columns, the moon overhead was unhelpfully bright, with visibility at about ten miles. As the vessels gathered off the Goodwins the smaller Coastal Motor Boats and launches began tearing through the water like children desperate to start their journey, and the destroyers, their latent power in check, called through their safety valves that they also wanted to get down to business. The centre column was led by *Vindictive*, with *Daffodil* and *Iris* in tow, followed by the five blockships, two of which were to head for Ostend. Commander Alfred Carpenter was in command of *Vindictive* and was also responsible for navigating the entire armada to its destination. The starboard column was led by *Warwick* and three other destroyers, with submarines C1 and C3 in tow. The route across the Channel ended at Position G, from where the ships would separate to undertake their individual tasks. The clear weather had changed during the crossing and had become foggy with a steady rain falling.

Timing was the key: first *Vindictive* had to reach and secure the Mole, drawing the attention of the defences, followed within minutes by the submarines blowing up the viaduct section to prevent reinforcements getting onto the Mole, and while all this was taking place, the blockships were to round the end of the Mole, pick their way through the booms and head for the canal, where they would be sunk. The time for the final approach had arrived and, as *Vindictive* set off for the Mole, the wind direction changed. This meant that the smokescreen could not hide the cruiser from the German batteries.

Increasing the ship's speed to its maximum, Commander Carpenter, who had navigated the entire armada across the Channel, now prepared *Vindictive* to run the gauntlet. As the Mole came into sight the enemy guns opened fire and, with the ship illuminated by star shells, the German gunners simply could not miss. The guns on *Vindictive* replied, but the ship was coming under a murderous rate of fire. Most of the damage was to the upperworks and several of the ship's guns and their crews were destroyed as

There are a number of artists' impressions of the attack on the Zeebrugge Mole. This one is by German artist Willy Stüwer.

were the special flame-throwers designed by Commander Brock. At one minute past midnight on St George's Day, 1918, HMS *Vindictive* struck the outer wall of Zeebrugge Mole with her specially designed fenders.

As the ship came alongside it was discovered that, of the eighteen special gangways built to take the storming parties onto the wall, all but two had been destroyed by enemy shells. The plan was for *Vindictive* to anchor alongside the wall, but the port anchor was jammed and, when the starboard anchor was lowered, it resulted in the ship swinging away from the wall, making it impossible for even the two remaining gangways to be used. There was nothing that *Vindictive* could do and, as she swung helplessly, the German shore batteries began to pound her remorselessly.

Onto this desperate scene there suddenly arrived out of the gloom HMS *Daffodil*. On the final approach to Zeebrugge the towing hawsers for her and *Iris* had parted and there was no knowing whether they would be able to complete their missions, but, not a moment too late, the little ship, under Lieutenant H G Campbell, came steaming straight at *Vindictive* and shoved her bodily alongside the Mole wall. The two serviceable gangways were at once lowered and the order rang out to 'Storm the Mole'. The first task of the storming parties was to secure *Vindictive* to the Mole with specially designed grappling anchors (one of which can today be seen near to Dover War Memorial), but a combination of the lurching of the ship and damaged machinery made this impossible. The only option was for *Daffodil* to carry on with her duties as a tug until the mission was completed. This she did, despite coming under constant fire, during which Campbell was shot in the face. Now that *Vindictive* was secured, her remaining guns opened up on their targets; the Mole batteries came in for special attention and the specially installed howitzers, operated by crews of the Royal Marine Artillery, pounded the shore guns.

The storming parties made their precarious way over the gangways and onto the Mole. As they were doing so, there was a sudden and massive explosion to the west. The sky was lit up and flames rose hundreds of feet into the air. Had the submarines succeeded in their attack on the viaduct? The seamen storming the Mole were now being led by Lieutenant Commander Adams and, as he could do no more with his flame-throwers, Commander Brock decided to join the attack. There is no hard evidence about Brock's fate, but he was last seen, revolver in hand, running into an enemy hut. His body was never found. It was later revealed that when Arthur Brock had boarded the *Vindictive*, he had brought with him a box marked 'Highly Explosive. Do Not Open'. The box contained several bottles of vintage port for his men. Hearing of his death, an old friend said, 'He was the sort of man who would never dream of going back. I can imagine him being on the Mole at Zeebrugge and, if he lost his revolver, fighting with his hands.'

As the bluejackets climbed over the parapet wall they came under heavy machine-gun fire from trenches below them. A bombing party was sent to destroy the position, but found it defended with barbed wire and many fell as they came under cross-fire from German vessels anchored within the harbour. Commander Adams left his men under cover and returned to gather reinforcements. Lieutenant Commander Arthur Harrison, an old Dover College pupil before he joined the Royal Navy, decided to act. He had earlier been struck in the head by a piece of shrapnel and suffered a broken jaw, but he realized how critical this moment was and, gathering a party of men, prepared to attack the machine guns. He led the charge along the parapet into the face of heavy machine-gun fire; he and all but two of his men were mown down. Commander Carpenter later wrote 'Harrison's charge down the narrow gangway of death was a worthy finale to the large number of charges which, as a forward of the first rank, he had led down many a rugby football ground.'

One of the two survivors of Harrison's party was Able Seaman Albert McKenzie. He was injured but, Lewis gun blazing, he continued forward until the gun was shot from his hands. Undaunted, he scrabbled for a revolver and a rifle with its bayonet fixed and picked himself up to resume his single-handed assault. McKenzie reached the German trench, where he set about 'pushing, kicking and kneeing every German who got in the way. When I was finished I couldn't climb the ladder so a mate of mine lifted me up and carried me up the ladder and then I crawled on my hands and knees inboard.' Although he survived the Zeebrugge attack, and the war, McKenzie succumbed to the post-war influenza outbreak and died in 1919. He was just nineteen years old.

As the fierce, often hand-to-hand, fighting was taking place on the Mole, the other Mersey ferry, *Iris*, was in serious trouble. Under the command of Commander Valentine Gibbs, she had reached the Mole wall some distance from the *Vindictive*. The plan was then to secure her to the wall with parapet anchors and disembark the demolition parties using scaling ladders. The swell of the sea was hampering the job, and after several attempts to secure the ship had failed, Lieutenant Claude Hawkings had the men hold one of the ladders upright as he ran up and leapt onto the Mole. As he did so, the ladder hit the wall and was smashed to pieces, but Hawkings sat astride the wall ready for an anchor to be thrown up at him. Suddenly he came under fire from Germans and, though firing back with his revolver, he stood no chance and was cut down. Lieutenant Commander George Bradford was in overall charge of the demolition party on board *Iris* and, seeing the mission

HMS Vindictive *back in Dover Harbour after the Zeebrugge raid.*

in jeopardy, he climbed one of the ship's derricks which was being pounded against the Mole wall. Waiting for the right moment, and holding an anchor, he launched himself at the wall. Miraculously, he landed safely and was in the process of securing the anchor, when a nearby machine gun opened fire and riddled him with bullets. As he fell into the sea, another officer dived in to save him but, despite attempts to rescue them, both men perished and were swept away.

Above the din of battle came the sound of a ship's siren. It was the letter 'K' in Morse, the signal for the storming parties to withdraw. Commander Gibbs on *Iris* put the ship about and, still under heavy fire, made for *Vindictive*, where she might find some protection. Almost immediately *Iris* received a direct hit, and the shell exploded between decks causing carnage among the crew. Another shell burst in the wardroom, which was being used as the sick bay, with more loss of life. Above decks, yet another shell had destroyed part of the bridge and caused a serious fire. Somehow *Iris* remained afloat and her engines kept turning, but when a motor boat arrived to provide her with a smokescreen, she disappeared from view. At 2.45 pm on the afternoon of St George's Day, under command of Lieutenant Oscar Henderson, *Iris* sailed into Dover. Somehow she had managed to limp across the Channel under her own steam. The welcome from those waiting at Dover was ecstatic but, the survivors on board *Iris* carried with them the sad cargo of 77 dead shipmates, including Commander Valentine, and another 105 wounded.

The second part of the diversionary attack on Zeebrugge was the destruction of the viaduct connecting the main part of the Mole to the land. Two redundant submarines, C1 and C3, were fitted out at Dover and packed full of high explosives. Of all the elements of the attack, this was considered the most dangerous, and for this reason all the crew members were volunteers. To give the crews at least some chance of survival, the vessels were each equipped with a form of remote control.

With their skeleton crews of a commander, another officer and four seamen, the journey across the Channel should have been straightforward: the submarines were to be towed across. Unfortunately, C1's towing hawser separated and she was unable to take any part in the attack. Everything depended upon C3, under the command of Lieutenant Richard Sandford. As C3 slipped silently towards the viaduct, the time was approaching 12.15 am, and the fighting on the Mole had already begun. Under the glare of the star shells and gunfire, the German defenders spotted C3 and she fell under the glare of a searchlight. Perhaps because they thought she was friendly or because they thought they might catch her intact if she collided with the viaduct, C3 was subjected to only brief gunfire. Sandford set course for the viaduct, approaching at a right angle. It soon became clear that it was a British submarine and it was heading full speed at the viaduct. Too late the enemy fire resumed, including automatic fire from men on the viaduct itself. The crew should now have engaged the remote control, set the time fuses and abandoned C3 to her fate, but instead they chose to manually navigate the submarine right into the target. The impact was so great that C3 was lifted bodily out of the water and was wedged firmly in the perfect position. The crew lowered a small motor boat and, as Sandford set the fuses, they abandoned ship, ready to make a quick departure. They then discovered that the propeller was damaged. Taking up the oars which had – thankfully – been provided, the men rowed for all they were worth, still under constant fire from the Germans, who wounded both Sandford and the other officer. The little boat was hit several times but the water pump managed to keep it afloat. Having pulled themselves 300 yards clear, the men were rewarded by the spectacle of C3 exploding, taking a large chunk of the viaduct with her. Shortly afterwards the crew of C3 were picked up by a picket boat commanded by Sandford's brother, whose sole task that night was to rescue the submarine crews if, against the odds, they survived their ordeal.

The events described so far were, of course, secondary to the main purpose of the attack on Zeebrugge – the sinking of the three blockships. To clear the way, and to create added confusion among the defenders, two high-speed Coastal Motor Boats (CMBs) were detailed to precede the blockships into the harbour. CMB7 was first in and, spotting a German destroyer at anchor, fired a torpedo, which exploded near the forebridge. Her job done, and being under constant fire, it was time for CMB7 to leave. Pursued by several small enemy boats, her superior speed would have got her clear, but suddenly CMB7 struck an unlit buoy, putting a hole in her bows. In danger of sinking, she set off again and managed to keep up a speed which kept the bows clear of the water – until the engine failed. Again in danger of sinking, CMB7 was spotted by a British destroyer, taken in tow, and arrived safely back at Dover. CMB5 had followed her sister vessel into the harbour and had also torpedoed a destroyer, before making her getaway.

In line astern, *Thetis*, *Intrepid* and *Iphigenia* made for the extremity of the Mole, looking for the rockets from *Vindictive* which would be the signal to make their turn and enter the harbour. Just ahead of them the destroyer HMS *North Star* was patrolling. There is little doubt that the presence of the destroyer drew much of the attention of the Germans, which might otherwise have fallen on the blockships. *North Star* had already exchanged torpedoes with an enemy ship, both missing their mark, when she arrived just east of the end of the Mole. Firing off another torpedo at an anchored ship, *North Star* was then illuminated by searchlights and came under heavy fire from German batteries. Undeterred, she fired three more torpedoes at anchored ships, but shells continued to fall and *North Star* took hits to the engine room and boiler rooms, which effectively crippled her. To her aid then came HMS *Phoebe*, fresh from rescuing the crew of the submarine C3. Putting out a smokescreen, *Phoebe* made several attempts to tow and push *North Star* out of trouble, with shells landing on both ships causing mounting casualties and damage. After a struggle lasting forty-five minutes, *North Star* had to be abandoned and her crew taken on board *Phoebe*.

If the crews of the blockships hoped that all the attention being given to the two destroyers, along with the fighting on the Mole, would divert attention from them as they entered the harbour, they were to be disappointed. *Thetis* was first to enter, but she immediately became fouled in the boom nets and slowed to a stop. The Mole guns which had not been put out of action and the shore batteries could not miss, and shells poured into the stricken ship. There was a silver lining to the fate of *Thetis*: first, when she had torn through the boom nets she had created a large gap through which her sister ships were able to steam, and, secondly, the German guns seemed to ignore *Intrepid* and *Iphigenia* as they made their

The crew of HMS Vindictive *after the raid. Captain Carpenter is at the front with his arm in a sling.*

way to the canal mouth. Lieutenant Bonham-Carter of *Intrepid* headed for his target and, having reached it, he turned the ship so that it was wedged across the width of the canal. Ordering his crew to abandon ship, he set off the charges which blew out her bottom. A little way behind, *Iphigenia* was coming under attack and her commander, Lieutenant Billyard-Leake, called for full power as he saw a chance to thread his ship past *Intrepid* and get further into the canal, a feat which he managed, before he too ordered his crew to the boats and sank *Iphigenia*.

There were now the crews of the three blockships marooned inside Zeebrugge Harbour, waiting and hoping that they would be rescued. For this purpose high-powered motor launches had been included in the armada. ML526 was first into the fray, picking up many of the crew of *Thetis*, while ML282 rescued the last men to leave the ship, Lieutenant Bonham-Carter, an officer, and four petty officers. These two motor launches then set about locating the crew of *Intrepid* and *Iphigenia*. The entire operation was carried out under fire and, missions completed, the boats made good their exit from the harbour. ML526, with sixty-five survivors on board, made it back to Dover under her own steam, while ML282, having sustained severe damage, as well as the loss of one officer and two of her four seamen, passed her cargo over to HMS *Warwick*.

Wing Commander Frank Brock (left) and Lieutenant Commander Arthur Harrison. Both took part in the raid, and were among those who perished.

Photograph taken from a British reconnaissance aircraft after the raid showing the positions of the three blockships.

It was now time to go home. HMS *Vindictive* cast off from the Mole a little over an hour after she had arrived, taking with her a large chunk of the wall, which had become lodged in her mangled upperworks. With her consorts, *Iris* and *Daffodil*, the slow process of withdrawal began, with the German gunners hoping to deliver fatal blows as the ships' hulls came into sight. But they were to be disappointed: Commander Brock's smoke-making apparatus was now put to the ultimate test and it did not fail, as the ships disappeared behind an impenetrable cloud of fog. The battered ships headed back to Dover. Some needed help to get home, such as *Daffodil*, taken in tow by the destroyer HMS *Trident*. As each vessel arrived back at Dover, cheers went up, before the task of removing the dead and wounded began. As for the men who could still stand, they could have passed as pirates, with their tattered clothes and blackened faces. The raid had cost the lives of 214 British servicemen and another 383 were wounded. Of the dead, sixty-six were buried at St James's Cemetery in Dover.

Debate continues about the value of the Zeebrugge Raid in terms of hindrance to the German U-boat operations, but of one thing there is no doubt – at a time when Britain had its back against the wall on the Western Front, the news of such a daring attack created a massive boost to morale at home and abroad.

In 1919 the King of the Belgians presented the town of Dover with a bell. It had been removed by the Germans from a church and installed on the Zeebrugge Mole to be rung in the event of an attack. This bell now hangs outside the Maison Dieu and every year, on St George's Day, it is rung by the Mayor of Dover. The final chapter in the Zeebrugge story happened in 1945, when Admiral Keyes, the man who had led the raid, died, and after a service at Westminster Abbey was brought to Dover for burial alongside his men.

Chapter 8

Peace Returns

When the guns fell silent at 11 am on 11 November 1918, the country erupted, with church bells ringing, firework displays and the Royal Family appearing on the balcony at Buckingham Palace. However, in contrast to the speed with which the country moved from peace to war in 1914, the transition back to peace took far longer, and was just as traumatic. Those most obviously affected by the slow process of recovery were the widows and families of men killed or wounded, and of course the men who did return often carried scars both visible and invisible. But it is sometimes overlooked that even the politicians were still picking up the pieces from the war long after it had ended. For instance, at the end of April 1921, the premiers of Britain and France met at Sir Phillip Sassoon's house at Lympne, just outside Hythe, to discuss the continuing delay by Germany in making reparations. France was all for sending troops into the Ruhr Valley, but Lloyd George told Briand that Britain did not have enough men to support such a move.

Folkestone

As in the rest of the country, the church bells rang out, blackout curtains were torn down and street parties were hurriedly arranged. However, after the first few weeks of celebration, serious problems began to set in. These problems were replicated at other towns, but Folkestone was the focal point and, during January and February 1919, there was a very real danger that what happened there could have sparked a revolution such as that taking place in Russia.

The problem had its roots in several issues which were causing general unrest among British troops. Despite the end of the conflict, the government continued with conscription, and for those to be demobilized the process was painfully slow and seen by many as unfair. The Derby scheme meant that 'ticket men', those who had a job to go to, should be demobbed first. As they were often the most recent conscripts, it meant that those who had served the longest were put to the back of the queue. There

The street party in Dover Street, Folkestone, to celebrate the announcement of the Armistice.

was also resistance at being sent back to France or, even worse, Russia, where Britain had taken sides against the Bolsheviks. Put simply, the men had done enough fighting and just wanted to go home.

Everything came to a head when a group of leave men arrived in Folkestone in January 1919. Already in the town there were several thousand men within the rest camps, waiting either for demob or to be sent abroad for further duty. It was on 3 January 1919 that a spark fell into the tinderbox of unrest and set off a full-scale mutiny. Despite heavy censorship of the events, the *Daily Herald* managed to get the story into print:

> On their own signal – three taps of a drum – two thousand men, unarmed and in perfect order, demonstrated the fact that they were fed up – absolutely fed up. Their plan of action had been agreed upon the night before: no military boat should be allowed to leave Folkestone for France that day or any day until they were guaranteed their freedom. It was sheer, flat, brazen, open and successful mutiny. Pickets were posted at the harbour. Only Canadian and Australian soldiers were to be allowed to sail – if they wanted to. As a matter of no very surprising fact they did not want to. One officer tried to interfere. He leapt across the gangway and got a rough-house.

Meanwhile troop trains were arriving in Folkestone with more men returning from leave and on their way to France. They were met with pickets ... in a mass they joined the demonstrators.

On Saturday an armed guard of Fusiliers was posted at the quays by the Army authorities. They carried fixed bayonets and ball cartridges. The pickets approached. One rifle made a show of going up: the foremost picket seized it, and forthwith the rest of the guard fell back. The mutineers visited the station in a body, after having posted their own harbour guards, and tore down a large label marked 'For Officers Only'.

On Saturday a great procession of soldiers, swelled now to about 10,000, marched through the town. Everywhere the townspeople showed their sympathy. At midday a mass meeting decided to form a soldiers' union. They appointed their officials and chose their spokesmen.

The men at Folkestone were supported by some 4,000 troops at Dover, who held a mass meeting in the Harbour Station and selected a deputation to meet the authorities. They then marched on the Town Hall and formed lines on either side of the road, overflowing into the side streets. The mayor had to admit them into the Town Hall, where a piano was provided for their entertainment. Nearby a cinema was opened for the soldiers to enjoy a free film show. In Hythe several hundred men from the School of Aerial Gunnery marched on the Hotel Imperial, where the officers were based.

Resolution of this explosive situation was achieved by concessions being offered by the politicians, much to the chagrin of the military commanders,

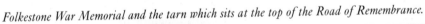

Folkestone War Memorial and the tarn which sits at the top of the Road of Remembrance.

some of whom, including Haig, wanted the ringleaders to be shot. By the middle of 1919 the demob process was almost complete, and the men who, as well-organized bands of armed soldiers, presented a serious challenge to the government had returned home to discover that 'the Land fit for Heroes' was not what they expected, but by then they had lost their bargaining power.

Official Victory celebrations took place across the nation in July 1919, and in Folkestone plans for the erection of a War Memorial were unveiled. Prominently placed on the eastern end of the Leas, outside the municipal offices, the memorial was joined shortly afterwards by a tarn at the top of Slope Road, which had been renamed Road of Remembrance. The tarn, surrounded by rosemary bushes, carried the inscription:

ROAD
OF
REMEMBRANCE

During the Great War tens of thousands of
British soldiers passed along this road on their way
To and from the front in Europe

Many towns were offered mementoes of the war, and Folkestone accepted a tank, which was displayed for some years at the Durlocks. Also offered was a Gotha bomber but, believing that it would cause distress to so many who had lost loved ones in the 1917 raid, this offer was declined.

Many towns were given a tank after the war. The Folkestone tank sat overlooking the town from the Durlocks.

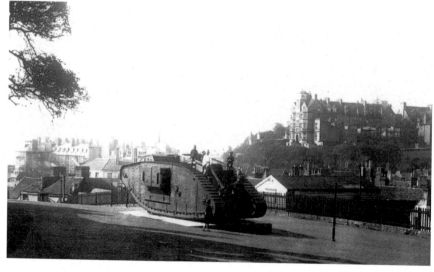

Dover

The end of the war for Dover signalled the beginning of a period of considerable activity, some of it parochial and some of national interest. For the South-Eastern & Chatham Railway, the first concern was to take back into service the vessels which had been commandeered by the Admiralty, and to resume cross-channel passenger services. Some ships, such as *Queen* and *Onward*, had been lost and others, such as the seaplane carriers *Riviera* and *Engadine*, had been so altered that they were unlikely to be capable of further use as passenger vessels. But the fleet had performed well: as well as tons of mail and stores, it was calculated that South-Eastern & Chatham Railway vessels had conveyed well over six million passengers between England and France and Belgium. The hospital ships had berthed at Dover on 3,166 occasions. On 18 January 1919 the service from Dover to Ostend was resumed with the opening to the public of the Marine Station.

As well as taking its toll on the ships of the South-Eastern & Chatham Railway, the war had claimed the lives of 556 railwaymen who had joined the services. On 28 October 1922 a memorial to these men was unveiled at Dover Marine Station (now Dover Cruise Terminal).

The activities of the Dover Patrol had been so prominent in the town that it was clear that its presence should also be marked. On 12 December 1918, at a ceremony at the Town Hall, the Mayor, E W T Farley, presented the Honorary Freedom of the Borough to Vice-Admiral Sir Roger Keyes, and

The street party in Victoria Street, Dover.

Dover welcomes Field Marshal Earl Haig, the British army commander on the Western Front.

also launched the Dover Patrol War Memorial Fund. In July 1921 the memorial at Leathercote Point near St Margaret's Bay was unveiled. It might seem curious that the spot chosen was so far outside the town. Certainly it commands excellent views of the Channel, but that is not the reason for the location of the memorial – it was built very near to the spot where, on 20 May 1918, the very last bomb was dropped on British soil during the Great War.

Dover played a key role in two solemn ceremonies, one on 13 May 1919, when the body of Edith Cavell was returned to England, and the other, on 10 November 1920, when the body of the Unknown Warrior was brought home for burial at Westminster Abbey.

Edith Cavell was born in 1865 in Norfolk and qualified as a nurse. Before the war she went to work at a hospital in Brussels and, when Belgium was overrun by the Germans, she chose to remain to nurse wounded soldiers. In September 1914, with the help of the resistance, Edith helped two British soldiers to escape, and she continued to play a central role in the escape network. It was only a matter of time before the Germans became suspicious, and in August 1915 she was arrested with twenty-six other suspects. At the trial in October 1915 Edith and four others were sentenced to death by the military court. Edith Cavell was executed by firing squad in Brussels on 12 October 1915.

The decision was made to bring Edith's body home for burial at Norwich

Cathedral. A train took her to Ostend where, on 13 May 1919, the coffin was taken aboard the destroyer HMS *Rowena*. Accompanied by HMS *Rigorous*, the *Rowena* entered Dover Harbour at 5.45 pm. The dockyard tug *Adder* and a lighter brought the flag-draped coffin to the Admiralty Pier, together with many wreaths and the party of relatives accompanying the body. It was met by the naval and military commanders and their staffs, placed on a wheeled bier and covered with a Red Cross flag. At the pier head, the coffin was put on a hearse accompanied by sixteen pall bearers from the women's nursing and other services. With a military guard the procession moved along the seafront to the Marine Station, where a carriage had been prepared and into which the coffin and wreaths were placed and hung with drapes. It stood there overnight, with a guard provided by the Buffs.

As the train headed for London and a memorial service at Westminster Abbey, crowds lined the route. *The Times* reported that 'at almost every station along the line and at windows near the railway and by the bridges

there were crowds of children quietly and reverently watching the passing. Schoolboys and schoolgirls in bright summer clothes had been brought by their teachers to the rail side and stood in long lines three and four deep on the platforms.'

A similar scene took place the following year when, from the great battlefields of France and Flanders, the body of an unknown soldier was exhumed to be reburied alongside the nation's great warriors and leaders at Westminster Abbey. This time it was the destroyer HMS *Verdun*, with an

The arrival of the Unknown Warrior at Dover in 1920.

escort of six more destroyers, which brought the coffin to Admiralty Pier, where military and civic leaders escorted it to a waiting train. The cliffs of Dover were lined with crowds to welcome home the Unknown Warrior. The next day, 11 November 1920, the second anniversary of the signing of the Armistice, the coffin was carried through the streets of London and laid to rest in Westminster Abbey.

As well as hosting these solemn occasions, Dover also knew how to celebrate the peace. Described as the 'Pageant of Empire', the town's contribution to the national celebrations on 19 July 1919 were lavish. The centrepiece was a procession, led by mounted constables and four separate bands, of thirty-eight vehicles all decked out to illustrate some feature of the

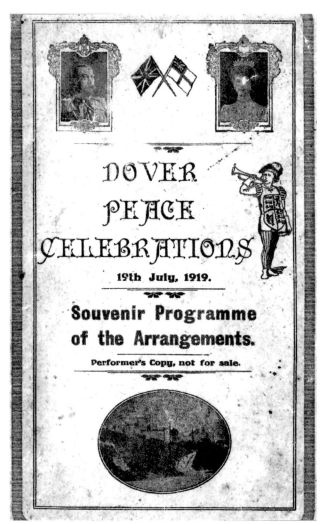

The official programme for Dover's peace celebrations in July 1919.

war, and including military and civilian services from all over the British Empire. Included in the parade were the Dover Anti-Aircraft Defence Command, the Royal Engineers complete with carrier pigeons, crews from the destroyers, and the RAF with a Fighting Scout Aeroplane. The Canadian tableau included Red Indians and cowboys, while the Indian vehicle carried a Maharajah with his retinue. Australia had dairymaids, South Africa had Boers and Zulus, and Egypt, of course, had Cleopatra and her slaves. The parade finished at the seafront opposite Waterloo Crescent, where hymns and national anthems were sung, rounded off with the Dover Triumph Song and 'Rule Britannia'. That evening there was a 'Grand Display of Fireworks, Searchlights and Illuminations', courtesy of the naval authorities.

Postcard Home

Dover – The Promenade.

To: Mr and Mrs J Powell, 65 Grantham Rd, Bradford Yorks
24th April 1919 Dover
Dear Mother and Father,
Just a line to let you know I have just arrived at Dover. We go to Clipstone this afternoon and hope to leave there in the morning (Friday) so I should be home tomorrow! The main thing is I am in Blighty!
  Love Harold xx

The Last Word

In Chapter 1 we recalled the first verse of a poem written by a soldier, George Willis, and addressed to his son. To George Willis we entrust the last word, being the final verse of that poem. Although his hope for an end to the catastrophe of war was not to be fulfilled, his sentiments must have echoed through every home where stood empty chairs or, perhaps worse, where sat men who had returned home but, crippled in mind or body, were strangers at their own firesides.

> You'd like to be a soldier and go to France some day?
> By all the dead in Delville Wood, by all the nights I lay
> Between our lines and Fritz's before they brought me in;
> By this old wood-and-leather stump, that once was flesh and skin;
> By all the lads who crossed with me but never crossed again,
> By all the prayers their mothers and their sweethearts prayed in vain,
> Before the things that were that day should ever more befall
> May God in common pity destroy us one and all!

Selected Bibliography

A number of contemporary and current local magazines and newspapers have provided valuable information. Additionally, many websites, both official and individual, have provided primary or supplemental information. It would be impossible to list all of them, and arbitrary to list just a few. However, one stands out as a beacon of local initiative which provides the local and family historian with an abundance of well-presented and reliable information and should be acknowledged: www.doverwarmemorialproject.org.uk.

A Pictorial and Descriptive Guide to Hythe, Sandgate and Folkestone (Ward, Lock and Co. Ltd, 1914)

Aspinall-Oglander, Cecil, *Roger Keyes* (The Hogarth Press, 1951)

Bacon, Admiral Sir Reginald, *The Dover Patrol, 1915–1917* (Hutchinson & Co., c.1920)

Beaupré, Diane, 'En Route to Flanders Fields: The Canadians at Shorncliffe during the Great War', in *London Journal of Canadian Studies* (2008)

Carlile, J C, *Folkestone during the War, 1914–1919* (F J Parsons, 1920)

Carpenter, Captain Alfred F B, *The Blocking of Zeebrugge* (Herbert Jenkins Ltd, 1921)

Castle, H G, *Fire over England: The German Air Raids in World War I* (Leo Cooper, 1982)

Collyer, David, *Flying: The First World War in Kent* (North Kent Books, 1982)

Coxon, Lieutenant Commander Stanley, *Dover During the Dark Days* (John Lane, 1919)

Easdown, Martin, and Genth, Thomas, *A Glint in the Sky* (Pen & Sword, 2004)

Emden, Richard van, and Humphries, Steve, *All Quiet on the Home Front* (Headline, 2003)

Firth, J B, *Dover and the Great War* (Alfred Leney and Co. Ltd, n.d.)

George, Michael, and George, Martin, *Coast of Conflict* (SB Publications,

2004)

Gould, David, *The South-Eastern & Chatham Railway in the 1914–1918 War* (Element Books, 1981)

Humphries, Roy, et al., *Wings over Kent* (Kent Aviation Historical Research Society, 1981)

Jerrold, Walter, *Highways & Byways in Kent* (Macmillan and Co. Ltd, 1908)

Jones, John, *Folkestone and the War* (1919)

Landau, Captain Henry, *Spreading the Spy Net: The Story of a British Spy Director* (Jarrolds, [1938])

Macdonald, Lyn, *1914–1918: Voices and Images of the Great War* (Penguin Books, 1988)

Mitton, G E, *The South-Eastern & Chatham and London, Brighton & South Coast Railways* (Adam and Charles Black, 1912)

Oak-Rhind, Edwin Scoby, *The North Foreland Lookout Post in the Great War 1915–1917* (Michaels Bookshop, 2005)

Poolman, Kenneth, *Zeppelins over England* (Evans Brothers Ltd, 1960)

Rosher, Harold, *In the Royal Naval Air Service* (Chatto & Windus, 1916)

Rudkin, Mable, *Inside Dover 1914–1918: A Woman's Impression* (Elliott Stock, 1933)

Smith, Victor, *Front-Line Kent* (Kent County Council, 2001)

White, C M, *The Gotha Summer: The German Daytime Air Raids on England* (Robert Hale, 1986)

Williams, Geoffrey, *Wings over Westgate* (Kent County Council, 1985)